WHY THIS BOOK WAS WRITTEN

I told my friend, the writer Jens Hansen, that I believed the Warren Commission Report to be a fable, a virtual insult to the intelligence of the American people. He asked me if I had ever considered letting someone help me write a book on the subject. I explained to him that we doctors who had worked on President Kennedy, whether out of respect or out of fear, had agreed not to publish what we had seen, heard, and felt.

Jens looked at me and said, "I know you've heard this a million times, and I don't want to sound like I'm preaching, but the American people have a right to know exactly what went on in Trauma Room 1, and exactly what you saw. Moreover, they have the right to know that their government was changed, that the course of history was dramatically altered in 1963 through a conspiracy to assassinate the President of the United States."

JFK HAS BEEN SHOT

CHARLES A. CRENSHAW, M.D.,
WITH JENS HANSEN
AND J. GARY SHAW

FOREWORD BY
ROBERT K. TANENBAUM

PINNACLE BOOKS
Kensington Publishing Corp.
http://www.kensingtonbooks.com

PINNACLE BOOKS are published by

Kensington Publishing Corp.
119 West 40th Street
New York, NY 10018

All Kensington Titles, Imprints, and Distributed Lines are available at special quantity discounts for bulk purchases for sales promotions, premiums, fund-raising, and educational or institutional use. Special book excerpts or customized printings can also be created to fit specific needs. For details, write or phone the office of the Kensington special sales manager: Kensington Publishing Corp., 119 West 40th Street, New York, NY 10018, attn: Special Sales Department, Phone: 1-800-221-2647.

Pinnacle and the P logo Reg. U.S. Pat. & TM Off.

ISBN-13: 978-0-7860-3427-7
ISBN-10: 0-7860-3427-0
First Kensington Mass Market Edition: October 2013

eISBN-13: 978-0-7860-3428-4
eISBN-10: 0-7860-3428-9
First Kensington Electronic Edition: October 2013

10 9 8 7 6 5 4 3 2 1

Printed in the United States of America

*To the residents and attending medical staff
of that era at Parkland,
and to Dr. G. Tom Shires, the "Chief."*

CONTENTS

Foreword by Robert K. Tanenbaum   ix

Introduction   1

Part 1:   The Beginnings   15

Part 2:   Friday—November 22, 1963   25

Part 3:   Updates 2013   205

Chapter 1:   Reflections by Jens Hansen   207

Chapter 2:   The *True* Fabricators Are
             Exposed by J. Gary Shaw   247

Chapter 3:   Personal Reflections on
             Charles Crenshaw and the
             JFK Assassination by
             Cyril Wecht, M.D., J.D.   290

FOREWORD

Introduction

When the government engages in an official inquiry into a matter of extreme public concern, the government is obligated, in good faith, to search for truth without fear or favor and report its findings to the people. Pursuant to this self-evident truth, the Warren Commission (WC) failed in its attempt to engage in a thorough, comprehensive and professional investigation into all aspects of the assassination of President John F. Kennedy. One of the central reasons for its abject shortcomings was that the Federal Bureau of Investigation (FBI), its primary responsible investigative agency, had prior to the WC investigation already concluded that Lee Harvey Oswald was the lone gunman and had acted without foreign intervention. The resulting WC alleged investigation was a sham, a charade that short-circuited a legitimate probe. Credible witnesses with vital evidence that contradicted the preconceived FBI conclusion were ignored. Dr. Charles Crenshaw's book demonstrates this critical failure. It gives credence to the public perception that the WC report was less than sincere in fulfilling its mission. Moreover, because of the overwhelming impact that the assassination had on our country, coupled with the WC faux investigation, overall government credibility suffered a stunning blow. I offer the following to suggest how and why it happened.

Analysis/Discussion

The Kennedy assassination was a colossal outrage. It fractured our fundamental belief in the orderly process of our political institutions. Camelot was shattered; and with it, all of its politically inspired romantic imagery vanished—its portrayal of a neo-idealism of truthful, just government analyses and pronouncements, constitutional equality, merit-based advancement and transparency of process disappeared.

The gut-wrenching events of November 22, 1963, in Dallas's Dealey Plaza paralyzed the nation. It was a political and personal catastrophe. We lost our President.

Shortly thereafter, within weeks, FBI Director J. Edgar Hoover proclaimed that the assassin, Lee Harvey Oswald, acted alone without foreign intervention. Case closed!

The government sought closure. The people demanded the truth. Portents of a winter of despair were about to dawn.

Over the years, the Kennedy assassination has receded into mythology and has become— like the tales of the Old West and the lives of secular saints such as Washington and Lincoln—fair game for the fabulist, the moralist and the entertainer. Libraries have been filled with books offering vying theories; some have been in support of the WC and some indignantly opposed. All postulate with passionate certainty the righteousness of their cause. To be sure, some treatises rise to the level of admirable scholarship. The most outstanding and valuable of those are narrations by the authors who actually played a significant role in the historical events.

Dr. Charles Crenshaw, a renowned surgeon with an acclaimed expertise in treating trauma victims, attended to President Kennedy in the emergency room inside Parkland Memorial Hospital just moments after the fatal bullets blasted through the president's head, causing his death. *JFK Has Been Shot* recounts in vivid detail those tempestuous, spellbinding percipient firsthand observations, analyses and medical procedures undertaken to try and save Kennedy's life. Dr. Crenshaw documented these events with a medical precision that memorialized an evidentiary foundation revealing tracks of bullets' entries and exits passing into and out of Kennedy's body and the condition of Kennedy's head wounds.

Dr. Crenshaw's participation inside Trauma Room 1 made him an important witness in the truth-finding process. Yet, this doctor and some of his colleagues who offered emergency care to the president and whose observations were corroborated and memorialized in writings and diagrams were *never* called to give testimony to the WC. In his book, Dr. Crenshaw informs as to the testimony in substance that he would have tendered. Most notably, based upon his expert findings, were his conclusions that the fatal shots, which killed Kennedy, entered the president's head and body from the geographical right front area (the grassy knoll) and not from the rear (the Texas School Book Depository building). Certainly, Dr. Crenshaw's expert testimony would have put into question the WC findings by contradicting its central theme that Oswald shot the president from the rear as the motorcade passed the depository building.

This extraordinary WC omission and failure to chronicle accurately the assassination events appears in other relevant areas as well. In so doing, the WC created a fog of deception that has substantially called into question its authenticity and credibility.

Why would the Commission not call Dr. Crenshaw, a highly credible expert whose opinions were invaluable in its alleged search for truth? And why did the Commission ignore trustworthy evidence and render conclusions to buttress a false narrative?

Certainly, if the WC was engaged in a virtuous search for truth, then there is no rational reason to omit Dr. Crenshaw and his corroborating evidence from the official record. However, if the WC was a facade devoid of investigative legitimacy designed to tailor its faux investigation to a predetermined conclusion, then one readily accepts the reality of its deception. The people expected a straightforward, fact-finding foray leading to historical truth. Instead, it was given a Lewis Carroll *Through the Looking-Glass* fantasy form of due process: first the sentence, then the trial. And if the accused is thereafter found not guilty, *"All the better!" says the Queen.*

In early 1977, I was deputy chief counsel to the congressional committee investigation into the assassination of President Kennedy. During the course of my probe, I came into possession of a memo dated November 23, 1963, from J. Edgar Hoover to all Bureau supervisory personnel. It stated, *inter alia* in substance, that the FBI agents who had questioned Lee Harvey Oswald for approximately seventeen hours immediately after Oswald's arrest had listened to a taped conversation between an individual who identified himself as "Lee Oswald" and an individual in the Cuban Embassy. The conversation originated inside the Russian Embassy in Mexico City by this faux Oswald, who telephoned the Cuban Embassy. The call was made on or about October 1, 1963, just about seven weeks before the assassination. The Hoover memo noted that the agents categorically concluded that the voice on the tape was not that of Lee Harvey Oswald. Based upon the evidence adduced during the investigation, I had reason to believe that David Phillips, the third-ranking member of the Central Intelligence Agency (CIA) in charge of Western Hemispheric operations, employed a *nom de guerre*, Maurice Bishop. Bishop had significant involvement with anti-Castro Cubans and Lee Harvey Oswald.

I had Phillips subpoenaed to appear before the House Select Committee on Assassinations (HSCA) in executive session. I asked him under oath where we could locate the tape of the so-called Oswald conversation of October 1, 1963, while inside the Russian Embassy in Mexico City. Phillips stated that it was CIA policy at the time to recycle the tapes every six or seven days and it was no longer in existence after the first week in October 1963. I then handed him the Hoover memo, which, according to the FBI director, clearly revealed that the tape was evidently available in Dallas on November 22 and 23, 1963. Phillips read the memo, then folded it, placed it in his jacket pocket, arose, and walked out of the hearing.

I immediately urged the committee to recall Phillips and advise him to obtain legal counsel so that he could be given an opportunity to purge potential criminal charges of contempt and perjury. Also, there were many more questions that he needed to answer. I further advised the committee of the urgency of the matter and gave them legal options. They chose to do nothing. Thereafter, our staff phones were denied long-distance telephone access, franking privileges (free mail service) were withdrawn, and staffers' pay was withheld.

Prior to my assignment with the congressional committee, I served as an assistant district attorney (ADA) in the New York County District Attorney's Office under legendary DA Frank Hogan. While there, I tried hundreds of cases to verdict. I was bureau chief of the criminal courts, ran the homicide bureau, and was in charge of the training program for the legal staff.

From experiences as a prosecutor, I knew well that there is no political way to investigate a case. There is no liberal or conservative way to gather evidence, and there is no Democrat or Republican way to evaluate it. Unfortunately, the congressional committee played politics with our investigation and subverted it. The members breached the trust reposed in them by the American people. They assured me that whatever the facts revealed would be forthrightly presented to the public. Regrettably, that was false.

Also, equally distressing, contrary to the credible facts, the WC made conclusive findings that Lee Harvey Oswald made that telephone call on October 1, 1963, in Mexico City inside the Russian Embassy to the Cuban Embassy. It too breached its duty to engage in an unconditional effort to report historical truth. For many reasons, the WC investigation was flawed.

Dr. Crenshaw's book presents the case for shots fired from the grassy knoll area situated in front and to the right of the president. Dr. Crenshaw offers his expert opinion with persuasive corroborating evidence. He memorialized it contemporaneously with his findings, as was his custom when treating victims of trauma. Yet, he was not called to give testimony before the Warren Commission. Read this truly thrilling, dramatically inspired page-turning account of the Kennedy assassination and be enriched with critically important historical truth.

Lest we fail to understand the state of mind of the WC commissioners and investigators, I offer this classic, documented exchange between WC commissioner Allen Dulles and Chief Justice Earl Warren, of the U.S. Supreme Court:

On or about the third week of January 1964,

Waggoner Carr, the attorney general of Texas, Dallas DA Henry Wade and Leon Jaworski, the chief counsel to Waggoner Carr, met with Chief Justice Warren in executive session. They informed him that from an "unimpeachable source" (their description) Lee Harvey Oswald was a contract employee of both the CIA and the FBI. The chief justice responded with an assurance that the information would be followed up with a fair inquiry.

"Not so fast," interjected Allen Dulles. The Chief Justice asked Dulles to explain. Dulles then stated in substance, "Well, if you ask J. Edgar Hoover if Oswald ever worked for the FBI, he will simply say no. After all, you know that he is already upset with us because he had early on concluded that Oswald was the lone gunman."

The chief justice inquired: "You mean that if I were to call an agent here as a witness under oath, he would lie?"

"Yes, if he were a good agent," said Dulles.

"Then who will he tell the truth to?" asked the chief justice.

"Maybe, maybe the president," replied Dulles.

Sadly, the WC treated this matter just as it did Dr. Crenshaw—it did nothing!

—Robert K. Tanenbaum
March 2013

INTRODUCTION

My name is Charles A. Crenshaw. I have been a surgeon for thirty years. Throughout my career I have watched thousands of gurneys slam through swinging doors of emergency rooms, carrying the old and the young, the rich and the poor, the broken and the dying.

Without exception, every time I have ever walked into an emergency room, I have encountered a victim of some unexpected calamity, the course of his life abruptly, sometimes permanently, interrupted. Terror, fear, remorse, shock, anger, and disbelief are but a few of the emotions that characterize trauma patients and their families. Helping these people is my business.

Trauma is ignored by most people, especially the young and rich who have no concept of life-threatening measures when they are well, when life is going their way. As the greatest killer of America's youth, trauma viciously and ruthlessly takes lives by stealth. Every day, each of us is exposed to myriad conditions that can subject us to severe injury, whether it be from an automobile accident, a fall on the ice, an injury in a sporting event, or a knifing or shooting. Trauma is not respectful of age, race, sex, occupation, or status.

Over the years, the faces of the many victims I've treated have blended into an indistinct obscured visage of pain, fear, and death. After so many cases, all my trauma patients seem as one, except for two—John Fitzgerald Kennedy and Lee Harvey Oswald.

The assassination of President Kennedy, the wounding of Governor Connally, and the murder of Lee Harvey Oswald were, in medical terms, classic cases of devastating trauma, specifically, hemorrhagic shock caused by profuse bleeding. One moment, the President and Governor were riding in a motorcade through downtown Dallas on a beautiful, sunny day, waving happily to the crowd. Only minutes later, they were at Parkland Hospital, mortally wounded, fighting for their lives. It was sudden. It was unexpected. And it was life altering. As for Oswald, he believed that he was securely in the custody of the Dallas Police Department. Then, in a fraction of a second he felt a sharp pain in his abdomen, and the American people had witnessed their first-ever murder live on their television sets.

Enormous damage was done to these men by the bullets that ripped through their bodies. The entire right hemisphere of President Kennedy's brain was obliterated, almost every organ in Oswald's abdomen was ravaged, and Governor Connally almost died from the missile that traversed his chest, arm, and leg.

Trauma can attack psychologically as well as

physically. When it does, its effects can be paralyzing and long lasting. Today, families of the assassination victims, the citizens of Dallas, the medical personnel at Parkland Hospital, and those of us who remember still feel the sting and the reverberations from the hail of gunfire that lasted for only a few seconds that fall day in 1963.

Compared with other events and incidents in my life, treating the President of the United States, as he lay fatally wounded, and then operating on the man who allegedly shot him, is like matching a magnificent ocean against an insignificant pond. Never, in my wildest imagination, did I consider that as a resident surgeon at Parkland Hospital in Dallas, Texas, on that fateful November day in 1963, I would experience the most poignant moments of my entire life. Ironically, feverishly struggling to save the dim spark of life remaining in President Kennedy's dying body was only the beginning of a harrowing weekend that ultimately introduced me to a level of discretion we seldom discover, one that I have had to practice to protect my medical career, and possibly my life.

Southwestern Medical School, Parkland Hospital, and the U.S. government have never been overly subtle about their desire for us doctors to keep quiet and not divulge what we heard, saw, and felt that November weekend in 1963. From the time President Kennedy was wheeled into the emergency room, until the recent filming in Dallas of Oliver Stone's movie, *JFK*, the doctors who witnessed President Kennedy's death have always felt the necessity to continue what has evolved over the years as a conspiracy of silence. Just recently, a gag order was issued from Southwestern Medical School warning those doctors still on staff there not to confer with Oliver Stone about President Kennedy's condition when he was brought into Parkland. Despite the fact that President Kennedy was neurologically dead when he was taken from his limousine, both Parkland Hospital and Southwestern Medical School, partners in academic medicine, will always be defensive about losing the most important patient they had ever had.

Through the years, there have been a thousand instances when I have wanted to shout to the world that the wounds to Kennedy's head and throat that I examined were caused by bullets that struck him from the front, not the back, as the public has been led to believe. Instinctively, I have reached for the telephone many times to call a television station to set the story straight when I heard someone confidently claim that Oswald was the lone gunman from the sixth floor of the Texas School Book Depository, only to restrain myself—until now.

The hundreds of similar cases involving gunshots that I have seen and treated since 1963 have further convinced me that my conclusions about President Kennedy's wounds were correct. I know trauma, especially to the head. To this day, I do not understand why the Warren Commission did not interview every doctor in President Kennedy's room. The men on that commission heard exactly what they wanted to hear, or what they were instructed to hear, and then reported what they wanted to report, or what they were instructed to report.

Had I been allowed to testify, I would have told them that there is absolutely no doubt in my mind that the bullet that killed President Kennedy was shot from the grassy knoll area. I would have also informed the Warren Commission about the call I received from Lyndon Johnson while we were operating on Lee Harvey Oswald. President Johnson told me that a man in the operating room would get a deathbed confession from Oswald. The incident confounded logic. Why the President of the United States would get personally involved in the investigation of the assassination, or why he would take the inquest out of the hands of the Texas authorities was perplexing.

Not until two years ago did I seriously consider writing a book on this subject. While I was attending an open house at a friend's home in Fort Worth, I was visiting with my friend, Jens Hansen, a writer who was completing his first book. We had previously discussed the assassination of President Kennedy and the other events of that weekend, but this discussion was more intense. We were speculating as to the long-term effects of President Kennedy's death.

I told him that I believed the Warren Report to be a fable, a virtual insult to the intelligence of the American people. Having read almost every book that had been published on Kennedy's death, in addition to having had an intense personal experience with the case, I considered myself one of only a few men who could make that claim. He asked

me if I had ever considered letting someone help
me write a book on the subject. I explained to him
that we doctors who had worked on President Kennedy, whether out of respect or out of fear, had
agreed not to publish what we had seen, heard,
and felt. It was as if we were above that, as if what
we knew was sacred, as if to come forward with
our account would in some way desecrate our pro-
fession. To a degree, I think we were afraid of criticism. And if one of us had started talking, the
others would have gotten into the act; and sooner
or later, the finger-pointing would have begun.

Jens looked at me and said, "I know you've
heard this a million times, and I don't want to sound
like I'm preaching, but the American people have
a right to know exactly what went on in Trauma
Room 1, and exactly what you saw. Moreover, they
have the right to know that their government was
changed, that the course of history was dramatically altered in 1963, through a conspiracy to assassinate the President of the United States.

"You, above all other people, saw and experienced more that weekend than any other person
at Parkland Hospital. Every critical event and
important moment involved you. If you go to your
grave with this information, if you do not publish it,
the people who did this thing to me and to you, and
to every other American, will be that much more
protected. As a witness to one of the United States'
most significant events, you have a responsibility
and a duty to record what you know.

"By doing so, there will have been at least one
person who was there who will have helped to ex-

pose the greatest lie of our time. This is your chance to do something very meaningful with your life, something so important that it outweighs your thirty years as a physician. I promise you this," he said, smiling, "eventually, one of your fellow doctors will break ranks and talk. It's inevitable, and it might as well be you."

"You may be correct," I replied. "I've heard that appeal about a million times, but not quite as convincingly as you just put it. I'll think about it."

For more than a year, his words echoed in my mind. Since 1963, people had encouraged me to write about my knowledge of John F. Kennedy's death. But never before had I seriously considered doing so.

Night after night, in a dreaded rendezvous with the past, I graphically relived every moment of that weekend in 1963, in morbid detail. More often than not, I awakened in the dead of evening in a cold sweat, trying to drive away the gruesome images that were becoming clearer and more disturbing as time went on.

I was having a recurring image. In slow-motion memory, I walked by Jacqueline Kennedy, who was bloodstained and distraught, as I entered Trauma Room 1. As I approached, Dr. Jim Carrico and Dr. Malcolm Perry were feverishly working on President Kennedy. Beginning at his feet, I remembered every hair, mole, and wrinkle on the President's body. With each successive image, the bullet hole in his neck bubbling blood, and parts of the President's brain dangling from his skull increasingly took on more dimension and color. His struggle to breathe and the fading sounds of his failing heart tormented me.

Drops of his blood hitting the kick bucket beneath the gurney tolled the remaining seconds of President Kennedy's life, as the voices of Dr. Charles Baxter and Dr. Kemp Clark echoed those eternal words of doom. Looking into the somber faces of Dr. Malcolm Perry, Dr. Robert McClelland, and Dr. Ronald Jones as we all accepted the inevitable, then embracing Jacqueline Kennedy as Dr. Charles Baxter tenderly told her that her husband was dead, recomposed within me the emotional tenor of those terrible moments.

I relived the tactics of intimidation practiced by the Secret Service agents. The "men in suits," as we referred to them, struck fear into Parkland's personnel as the agents went about providing more protection and concern for a dead President than they had shown for a living President. I followed the heavily armed agents as their entourage surrounding the casket escorted President Kennedy's body out of Parkland Hospital, their arrogance almost palpable; Jacqueline Kennedy walked alongside, her hand resting on the coffin.

As the months passed, I continued to read and study every available publication on the subject, increasingly becoming more and more outraged at the great lie that had been perpetrated. For the first time, I questioned whether I had actually entered into a contract with the other doctors to not write my story. I hadn't taken an oath or signed an agreement to that effect. All I had done was fail to object openly to the edict of secrecy proclaimed in

Trauma Room 1 by Dr. Charles Baxter, professor of surgery and director of the emergency room, just after President Kennedy died. Silence cannot be taken to mean tacit approval.

Finally, on November 17, 1990, while sitting at my desk at Peter Smith Hospital, after reviewing the mounting evidence and my recurring memories one last time, I decided to tell my story. I realized that the compulsion to chronicle my account of that fateful weekend at Parkland Hospital in 1963 had begun to grow within me almost immediately after the assassination. I knew I had to speak out, if for no other reason, because the democratic process created by the greatest constitutional document ever written was being callously and maliciously circumvented by a handful of cowards. My silence has protected them. The choice of the American people was cast aside with one squeeze of a trigger. The work of men like James Madison, Alexander Hamilton, John Jay, Benjamin Franklin, and the sacrifice of the millions who have defended the Constitution, were rendered impotent by a few sorry criminals.

Efforts to suppress and distort the truth about the assassination on the part of government officials and agents, as well as certain representatives of the media, have been well documented in previous works on this subject. That these efforts included threats, intimidation, falsification and destruction of evidence, and even death, have played no small role in my silence of the past twenty-eight years. I am fifty-nine years old. My medical career is over, and I no longer fear the "men in suits" nor the criticism of my peers.

Several days later, I invited Jens Hansen to my home to tell him of my decision. When he arrived at my home in Fort Worth in the early afternoon, he left the car's motor running and came to my door. He asked me if I had time to make a trip to Dallas. Fifty-five minutes later we entered the JFK Assassination Information Center on the third floor of the West End Marketplace, at 603 Munger, just three blocks from the Texas School Book Depository Building in downtown Dallas.

Meeting us there was a man named J. Gary Shaw, who I quickly discovered is one of the world's top authorities on the Kennedy assassination. He has invested twenty-seven years and a small fortune into research and the investigation of every aspect of Kennedy's death. Through it all, he has amassed a vast source of information, much of which he has produced through personal interviews.

After we had toured the Kennedy exhibit, we followed Mr. Shaw into a room that held the Information Center's archives. He reached into a file drawer and withdrew a manila envelope. From it he removed several 8 × 10 photographs, handed them to me, and asked, "Does that look like the same body that you helped place in the casket at Parkland Hospital in 1963?"

I was amazed. They were pictures of President Kennedy's autopsy taken at the Bethesda Naval Hospital, Bethesda, Maryland. But the photographs showed a back of President Kennedy's head that was different from the wound I witnessed. They indicated a contrasting scenario, one that would support the theory of a lone gunman firing from the sixth floor of the Texas School Book Depository. One picture showed President Kennedy's neck at the point where the bullet had entered, the spot where Dr. Malcolm Perry had performed a tracheostomy at Parkland to help the President breathe. The opening was larger and jagged—significantly different from the way it had looked to me in Dallas. There was no doubt in my mind—someone had tampered with the body, or the photographs.

"Where did you get these?" I asked while I examined them.

"I'd rather not say, Dr. Crenshaw," Shaw replied.

After studying the pictures for several more moments, I said, "No, these aren't the same wounds I saw at Parkland. From these pictures it appears that someone performed some surgery on the President between the time his body left Parkland Hospital and when these photographs were taken."

"Doc," Hansen said, "Gary has the facts to corroborate your belief that there was more than one gunman, that President Kennedy was struck by at least three bullets, two of which entered the front of his body. If you're interested, he has agreed to provide us some critical information. For years, he's been waiting to work with one of the doctors in Trauma Room 1. He believes that one of the missing links to proving the conspiracy is the medical side of the assassination."

"It gets worse," Shaw said as he returned the photographs to the file drawer, then turned and faced me. "According to reports, you placed Kennedy in a bronze casket after he had been wrapped in white cloth. Witnesses have now come forward

to state that when Kennedy's body was delivered
to Bethesda, he was taken from a gray shipping
casket, not swaddled in white cloth, but instead
zipped in a body bag like the ones from Vietnam."

"I'm aware of that," I said. "In addition, Commander J. J. Humes and his cronies made about
twenty or so critical mistakes in their postmortem
examination. None of them were forensic pathologists or experienced in examining bullet wounds.
In my opinion, if Earl Rose, the pathologist at Parkland, had been allowed to perform the autopsy, and
report the results to the Warren Commission, the
outcome of that report would have been considerably different. And the photographs of President
Kennedy would have reflected the true nature of
his injuries. But of course, that is exactly why the
'men in suits' (members of the Secret Service detail) took President Kennedy's body out of Parkland
at gunpoint. They had their orders—orders from a
high official in our government who was afraid of
the truth."

At that meeting, Hansen, Shaw, and I committed
ourselves to writing a work that would impart to the
reader both the emotions of those days and the
facts as we could best relate them through my experiences. As the words quickly turned to page
after page, years of fear turned to anger. I soon
realized that this work had become a catharsis, re-
leasing a lifetime of frustration. It soon became evident to us that my story is another piece to the
mysterious puzzle, and that we should write this
account in the context of the big picture.

As a result, we asked Gary Shaw to join us in

this endeavor by providing historical facts based upon his years of research. By weaving threads of my personal and medical observations of those incredible events into the ever-growing fabric of historical truth, we hope that in some small way the veiled has become less obscured, the perplexing has become clearer, and the government's lone-gunman theory is exposed as a preposterous lie. Further, it is our wish that my story, presented in this format, contributes to the ongoing effort to expose the Warren Report as a feigned document.

The cover-up of the truth of that nightmare in Dallas has insulted all thinking Americans. By revealing details of the events that occurred, and the medical facts of the patients treated during those three days at Parkland Hospital in 1963, we hope to provide a new perspective on the assassination of President Kennedy, and the tremendous, yet frightening, efforts to cover it up.

From the beginning, writing this book has been a labor of love and an exercise in pride for all three of us. I was amazed at the vividness of the details of those days in 1963, which I had repressed all these interim years, and the emotions I had deeply buried. I cried from the sorrow. I laughed at the funny moments that had refused to surrender to the insanity of it all. And I cursed the men who had killed the President and the government that had covered it up.

Here is my account of those incredible three days at Parkland.

PART 1:
THE BEGINNINGS

Many of us have dreamed that history's grand scheme will involve us in some far-reaching role or experience, thrusting us into notoriety and dramatically changing our lives. In 1963, such a fate took hold of me while I was a resident surgeon working out of a county hospital in a town struggling to become a city, and for four incredible days ruthlessly shook me. When it had let go, I had passed through the nucleus of the most mysterious murder in U.S. history, the assassination of President John F. Kennedy. From that moment on, neither Parkland Hospital nor I would ever again be the same.

While growing up in Paris, Texas, I aspired to be a doctor due to the strong influence of my father, Jack Crenshaw, and our family physician, John Arch Stevens. After completing high school, and with the commitment to study medicine burning deeply within me, I attended Southern Methodist University in Dallas, where I excelled in their pre-med program and graduated with honors. After earning a Bachelor of Science degree, I entered Southwestern Medical School, a newly established institution that provided the doctors for its teaching partner, Parkland Hospital, also a relatively new facility. Never in my wildest imagination did I consider when I walked into that first class that I would one day be standing over the President of the United States lying in the Parkland emergency room, with the right side and rear portion of his head blown off. Nor did I envision operating on his alleged assassin, Lee Harvey Oswald.

Although I could have attended any medical school in the country, I chose the University of Texas branch in Dallas, because, not only was Southwestern the closest medical school, it was the most affordable. Tuition was only $150 a semester, excluding books. There wasn't any ivy growing on the walls, but it was a damn good school, just the same. It was there that Dr. G. Tom Shires, professor and chairman of the Surgical Department at Parkland, who we referred to as "the little Caesar of surgery," inspired me to become a surgeon. Dr. Shires had told me that a surgeon is an internist who can cut.

When I finished medical school, I spent one year as an intern in internal medicine at the Dallas Veterans' Hospital. Then in 1961, I took one of the five residency positions at Parkland, which immediately distinguished me and my fellow residents as being among the "cream of the crop," firmly placing us on the coveted path to academic medicine. Through my association with the divine (Dr. Shires), I felt anointed, as all his staff believed themselves to be. Dr. Shires had a way of subtly conveying the message that if you were on his team, you were on the best squad in medicine.

I was a confident doctor, as we all were—even arrogant, I suppose. Our lofty opinions of our abilities as surgeons were partly attributable to the way in which we had learned surgical procedures. The saying went, "See one, do one, teach one." There was a lot of competition among us, but we respected one another as physicians and surgeons and worked well as a team—esprit de corps. We believed we could provide the best medical care in the country.

But the hospital was nervous about the image of residents playing such a supreme role in its services, although it was true. As a result, certain med-school officials deliberately masked the major role that I and other resident surgeons played in the medical aspects of the Kennedy assassination, and the Warren Commission failed to obtain from us what would have been important testimony. I had experience with head wounds from high-powered rifles, and I definitely had an opinion about the trauma to Kennedy's skull, which was in conflict with the doctors who performed the autopsy. I can't speak for my fellow physicians who were in Trauma Room 1, but I wasn't about to rock the boat by broadcasting my thoughts on the President's death, which could have threatened my future in academic medicine, and as it now seems, possibly even my life.

Many people still hold to the misconception that President Kennedy was delivered to a group of ragtag country doctors whose medical expertise was limited to suturing cuts and treating sore throats. We didn't appreciate doctors from the eastern medical establishment inferring that the President didn't get superlative health care. The truth was to the contrary, as evidenced by the impressive careers of the staff and resident surgeons who were at Parkland Hospital's emergency room that day in 1963.

Dr. G. Tom Shires, who until recently was chief of surgery and dean of Cornell University Medical School in New York, is now chief of surgery at Texas Tech Medical School in Lubbock, Texas. Dr. Malcolm O. Perry, who until recently was professor of surgery and chief of vascular services at Vanderbilt University Medical School in Nashville, Tennessee, is now professor and chief of vascular surgery at Texas Tech University Medical School in Lubbock, Texas. Dr. James "Red" Duke, the surgeon who operated on Governor Connally, is professor of surgery and director of emergency services at the University of Texas Medical School in Houston, Texas. Dr. Charles R. Baxter and Dr. Robert N. McClelland are professors of surgery at Southwestern Medical School. Dr. Charles J. ("Jim") Carrico is chairman of the department of surgery at Parkland Hospital and Southwestern Medical School. Dr. Ronald Jones is chief of general surgery at Baylor Medical Center. And I am now clinical professor of surgery at Southwestern Medical School and director and chairman of the department of surgery at John Peter Smith Hospital in Fort Worth, Texas. If I had been wheeled into an emergency room, mortally wounded, I would have felt pretty confident knowing that a surgical team like this one was taking care of me.

I've often considered what would have happened if President Kennedy's motorcade had been traveling east when he was shot, because they would have gone to Baylor Hospital. Back then, Baylor wasn't a teaching facility, and its staff wasn't prepared for trauma. There would have been perhaps one resident surgeon there. Connally, who was closer to death than anyone actually realized, may very well have died. Today, Baylor is a fine trauma hospital with excellent surgeons.

During my first year of residency, I conducted research in a fellowship under Dr. Shires' supervision in which we made medical history by discovering that death from hemorrhagic shock (blood loss) can be due primarily to the body's adjunctive depletion of internal salt water into the cells. Research continued to be a paramount function at Parkland. Almost three decades later, Drs. Joseph L. Goldstein and Michael S. Brown at Southwestern Medical School would again make medical history by winning the Nobel Prize for their research into cholesterol metabolism. I consider Southwestern now among the top five medical schools in the country, and I believe Parkland Hospital to be one of the finest trauma facilities in the world.

In 1963, Parkland was a 550-bed hospital, located between Harry Hines Boulevard and Stemmons Expressway, five miles north of downtown Dallas. It served an area population of one million people. Out of the 300 residents and interns, there were 25 general surgical residents. Today, Parkland is a 760-bed hospital with 850 residents and interns.

Since its inception, Parkland has been a M.A.S.H. unit for Dallas County's war zone, primarily treating the indigent who have no health insurance and who lack the money to purchase health care from private hospitals. As such, many of the injured brought to Parkland's emergency room are drunk, belligerent, and sometimes violent. I knew when the moon was full by the number of victims who were brought in. On an average day 380 emergencies are treated. For years we doctors there referred to the trauma team as those who treated the "knife and gun club."

When John F. Kennedy came to Dallas, health care was very different from what it is today, especially in the treatment of trauma-related injuries. Ambulances were hearses equipped with a single tank of oxygen, and there were no emergency technicians. Blood from African-Americans was not allowed to be transfused into whites, and vice versa. Other hospitals in Dallas didn't want to treat trauma cases because they were a money-losing proposition. A hospital's entire annual budget for such care could be, and many times was, spent on a few patients. And there were no such programs as Medicare or Medicaid. Mostly, we were treating the poor and underprivileged. Given the choice, a person of any means would never have chosen to go to Parkland because of its reputation—that is, unless he was in need of trauma care, in which case Parkland Hospital substantially improved his chances for survival. Otherwise the selection would have been a private hospital.

The Dallas police were our best friends, because

they protected us when we had to treat someone who was spitting, hitting, biting, or kicking. We could handle the abusive language but not the physical attacks. Back in those days we got the violent patients under control very quickly and effectively. In some cases we used towel clips on their ears, and, of course, the scissorlike blades completely penetrated their flesh. Then we would attach the other end to the bed sheet. If they moved, it would pull their ears off. We did the same thing to their noses, but we weighted the clip with a one-pound ether can draped over an IV pole. It sounds cruel, but it was for the patient's protection, too. Sometimes there was no other way to keep someone still long enough to treat him. You can't suture a man's laceration if he's spitting in your eyes and jabbing his fist into your groin.

I will never forget the man who pulled a pistol on me in Trauma Room 4, which was off the beaten path and where the worst behaved were taken. We had to run the gurney into his abdomen until he dropped the gun. It was the wild, wild West of the medical world.

Working at Parkland as a second-year resident, I was almost always exhausted, irritable, and often ill. I was so used to this condition that, at one point, it wasn't until my eyeballs turned yellow that I realized I had hepatitis. We called residency the "black hole" because the doctors in it were struggling to escape, and the young physicians desiring to become surgeons were working to get in.

In addition to working the emergency room every other night, we served on elective surgery teams

A, B, and C, where we worked every third night. We always rotated every other day on trauma surgical teams I and II. I worked thirty-six out of every forty-eight hours, seven days a week in an atmosphere of bedlam, all for a mere $100 a month, leaving little time for my wife and child.

To stay abreast of ongoing research, I, like my colleagues, would rise at four o'clock in the morning and peruse the medical journals. Then I'd rush off to the hospital to check on the progress of my own research projects before beginning my surgical day. Under those conditions, treating patient after patient in a web of blood, pain, and death, eventually became an academic exercise for me and my fellow surgeons. It was paradoxical. We were skilled surgeons fighting to preserve life, yet the conditions under which we saw it made us increasingly irreverent toward it.

I've always considered myself a conservative Democrat. I remember the political atmosphere on the eve of November 22, 1963. In 1960, Richard Nixon won Dallas County, something a Republican presidential candidate hadn't done since Reconstruction. During the heat of that election, Bruce Alger, the first Republican congressman from Dallas since the Civil War, spat on Lyndon Johnson and his wife as they walked from the Baker Hotel to the Adolphus, while others screamed, "LBJ has sold out to the Yankee socialists." In the ensuing melee it took thirty minutes for the Vice President to cross the street.

One month before President Kennedy came to Dallas in 1963, a housewife who was part of an extreme right-wing group hit UN Ambassador Adlai Stevenson in the head with an anti-UN sign. As he fled through the protesting mob to his limousine parked outside the auditorium, someone spat upon him. Even after he was in the automobile, the crowd rocked the car in an attempt to overturn it.

If John Kennedy came to Dallas today, the city would warmly embrace him as their President. But in those days, the influence of extreme political factions, like the John Birch Society, made it appear that Dallas hated President Kennedy, not so much the man himself, but the person it perceived him to be. It wasn't that Texans wanted him dead— they just didn't want him as their President. We knew our European history pretty well, and like the founding fathers, we didn't want a king. He came across as royalty with his money, his lifestyle, his family, and his charisma—oh, that charisma that literally flowed from him. As I remember, the only politician in Texas who liked him was Ralph Yarborough.

Robert and Jacqueline had warned the President not to travel to Dallas, but he came down here anyway to soothe the ruffled feathers of the state Democratic party. Lyndon Johnson, John Connally, and Ralph Yarborough were all at one another's throats over the growing movement to dump Johnson in 1964 as the Vice President. Conservative Democrats and Republicans alike were deeply suspicious of the rich, liberal, arrogant, and Catholic President.

Where were you on November 22, 1963? Almost three decades ago, early on the morning of that historic day, I was in surgery, beginning yet another round in the war of medicine against mayhem. But this tour of duty would be different. It would inexorably thrust me directly into the path of a spellbinding drama. It was an adventure of which most people can only dream. It was a life-changing experience. When I walked into Trauma Room 1, I entered the halls of history.

PART 2:
FRIDAY—
NOVEMBER 22, 1963

Midnight

Hotel Texas—Fort Worth

President Kennedy and Jacqueline are at the
Texas Hotel in Fort Worth. They arrived from
Houston late the previous evening, reaching
the hotel at 11:50 P.M.

The President's Secret Service entourage
has gone to the Press Club for drinks. Finding that Texas law prohibits the sale of liquor
after midnight, they journey to an all-night
"beatnik" nightclub called The Cellar. This
night spot, which has no liquor license, has a
reputation for giving away drinks to lawyers,
politicians, policemen—anyone the owner
thought to be important or useful in a time
of need.

The owner of the club, Pat Kirkwood, is a
close acquaintance of Jack Ruby. Both men
employ strippers Tami True and Little Lynn.
Little Lynn will later become the recipient of

Ruby's alibi-establishing Western Union money order, wired only minutes before the Oswald shooting. Kirkwood's father is a partner in a Fort Worth gambling establishment with a close associate of Ruby, Lewis McWillie. McWillie, according to FBI documents, was a murderer and was employed by Cuban Mafia leader Santos Trafficante. Trafficante was a key figure in the CIA's plots to kill Cuban President Fidel Castro. Cellar-owner Kirkwood is himself an interesting figure. A soldier of fortune and pilot of his own twin-engine plane, he will fly to Mexico a few hours after the assassination.

Ten agents of Kennedy's protection detail take advantage of The Cellar's free alcohol until approximately 3:30 A.M. Four of these agents will be in the follow-up car behind the President at the time of the assassination. At The Cellar another three agents, assigned to guard to President's hotel suite, take their "coffee break" with their fellow agents, leaving two Forth Worth firemen in their place. These agents are overheard laughing and joking about leaving the protection of the President and First Lady in the hands of two firemen. Later, as the shots ring out in Dallas, only one of the President's detail makes any effort to protect the Chief Executive. Attempting to leave the follow-up car and aid the wounded President, he is ordered back by the special agent in charge.

Though Secret Service regulations governing a White House detail while in travel status prohibit the use of intoxicating liquor of any kind, and a violation or slight disregard is cause for removal from the Service, none of the agents involved will receive any disciplinary action.

In significant contrast to this security breach on the part of the President's protective personnel, none of the Vice President's Secret Service detail are involved in the drinking at The Cellar. In fact, they are in their rooms resting for the next day. Immediately after the first shot, LBJ's personal agent shouts "Get down" and vaults over the backseat, forcing the Vice President down and out of the line of fire.

4:00 A.M.

Hotel Texas—Fort Worth

The President will soon rise to begin another busy day, continuing his Texas tour to ameliorate the bitter feuding among top state Democrats. Scheduled events include a parade through downtown Dallas and a luncheon at the Trade Mart. There is still a degree of uncertainty as to whether Vice President Lyndon Johnson and Senator Ralph Yarborough, at odds over politics, will agree to ride in the same automobile.

Home—Dallas

When I opened my eyes, I still felt tired. I didn't need an alarm clock to awaken me every morning between 4:00 and 4:30, because I had become accustomed to doing it every day—every day that I slept, that is. It's amazing to me how I programmed myself to get up at that ungodly hour, day after day, although I was always exhausted. So much did it become a habit, that I still rise at that time every morning, some twenty-seven years later. It's like being on automatic pilot.

I knew President Kennedy was coming to Dallas, because I had read it in the *Dallas Morning News* the previous day. But I didn't think much about the President that morning. In my enclosed world at Parkland Hospital, I couldn't get out to see him. Parkland took the best of me and every other surgeon there, and threw back what was left of us to our families. Already, my marriage was showing signs of strain.

Politics, although interesting to me, was way down on my priority list. But my father and I knew Sam Rayburn, who was from Bonham, twenty-five miles from Paris, Texas. Through the newspaper I had kept up with the problems in the Democratic party at that time. Politically, Texas was a divided and hostile state. After witnessing what had transpired with other Democrats visiting Dallas, namely Lyndon Johnson and Adlai Stevenson, I feared that Kennedy's visit might also initiate an ugly incident.

After rubbing my eyes for several moments, I was able to focus on the bedroom window. The blinds were partially open, and I could see that it was still pitch black outside. I remember not getting to see the sun for days. Extended periods of arriving at the hospital before sunrise and leaving after it had set made it difficult to keep track of time. For a resident surgeon in a trauma hospital, working where there are no windows, there's no such thing as day and night—just periods of being on-duty and off-duty. It was going to be a very unusual day in that the surgical schedule was light—one cholecystectomy (gallbladder operation). Then I would take off in the middle of the afternoon, which was something even more unusual.

I struggled out of bed and staggered through the dark to the bathroom. My wife was still sleeping, as was my three-year-old son, Chad. I closed the door, turned on the light, threw some cold water on my face, squinted at the mirror through puffy eyes, and marveled at the thirty-year-old face that looked fifty that morning. "Oh, God! It's show time," I groaned.

In the autumn of 1963, I was off trauma and on elective surgery. As a resident, I headed surgical team B, which was on duty twenty-four hours every three days. When I was on trauma, which was six months at a time, I rotated every other day. Of course this was in addition to all my other duties, such as research and working with junior residents. During surgery, a staff surgeon, usually Dr. Shires or someone else on staff, assisted me. "Show time" simply meant that I was on stage every moment of every day, playing to the harshest critics imaginable. That's the way it was for a resident surgeon pursuing academic medicine. Unlike controlling a drunk in the emergency room, or practicing out of a private hospital, there was no privacy in the operating room of an academic hospital, especially for a resident surgeon in charge of a surgical team. The results of your work disseminated through the hospital's grapevine network so fast that there might as well have been a marquee posting it. If you screwed up, everybody in the place knew it before the patient was rolled into the recovery room.

At the root of this intense competition was the intense jealousy between the "town" and the "gown." Some doctors chose the town, which was private practice. But I preferred the gown, which to me meant being on the cutting edge of medicine. I'd rather command the *Pinta* than ride on the *Queen Mary*.

I lived at 4714 Bradford Drive, apartment A, which was a two-bedroom, two-bath place in a low-income apartment complex across from a housing project, five minutes from the hospital. My rent was $175 per month. Parkland paid me $150 a month, and I received an additional $200 each month from an NIH Research Fellowship. My parents supplemented my income to make up the difference so that I could feed my family.

In the apartment just across from our back door lived my brother-in-law, an orthopedic surgeon. Ronald Jones, my senior resident at Parkland, lived down the street. Medical personnel were segregated from other renters across the street in the low-cost housing project.

Parkland Hospital—Dallas

I got to the hospital that morning, a little before five o'clock. I remember how foggy and miserable it was as I walked from my 1959 Mercury. It looked to be a bad-weather day. For the first time that morning, my thoughts focused on the President's visit, as I thought how lousy a day it would be for a parade. Once in the building I went to the changing room on the second floor, where we did all the surgery, and put on a scrub suit and a white coat. Then I moved across the hall to the doctors' lounge and had my first cup of coffee, which was brewing twenty-four hours a day next to the operating rooms.

I then stepped down that same hall, by the anesthesia room and the recovery area through a set of double doors that led to the nurses' station in the surgical ward, which was 2-East. There, I pulled the charts on my patients to review their progress during the past few hours. I also examined the lab tests I had ordered the previous day.

The interns and senior medical students assigned to surgery conducted the tests and were responsible for knowing the laboratory results. I wanted the data before they got to the hospital. Then I would thoroughly quiz them.

When it came to supervising interns, students, and junior residents, I was considered one of the meanest sons of bitches in the entire hospital, because I insisted that they know and understand the importance of what they were doing at all times. Also, I wanted to look good because of the competition among the resident doctors. We were reviewed each year, and our performance was a matter of pride and promotion. It was gamesmanship. Actually, I wasn't nearly as bad as they claimed I was until my last year of residency, at which time my nature almost became malignant. If making a critical mistake was made traumatic enough for the perpetrator, I reasoned, he would not only remember it, but he would learn from it. I know that's true because some of the most valuable lessons I learned during my career were etched into my memory with disturbing revelation. I will always be indebted to my mentors who assiduously taught me surgery.

After writing orders and reviewing the lab results, I went down to the first floor and walked to the medical school, which is contiguous to the hospital. There I reviewed the progress on Doctors Shires' and Baxter's research projects. Then, before breakfast, I returned to the hospital and made rounds to look in on several critically-ill patients. At that point everything was going smoothly. With Dr. Shires, chairman of the surgery department, out of town, I felt relaxed and unpressured. I was looking forward to finishing the one surgical case and taking off that afternoon, which to me was tantamount to a Hawaiian vacation.

Having visited all my patients, I went to the dining room on the first floor, and was eating two hard-boiled eggs, toast, and coffee while reading the newspaper. The *Dallas Morning News* was full of information and stories about President Kennedy and the First Lady. In one of the articles there was a map showing the route of his motorcade through downtown Dallas. From Love Field he would be driven south down Harwood Street to Main, then west to Houston, back north to Elm, then out Elm to Stemmons Expressway, and back north to the Trade Mart for a scheduled luncheon.

With sickening clarity, I recall a full-page editorial purchased by an extremist group that viciously attacked the integrity of President Kennedy by claiming he was a Communist. The President was posed in a frontal and side mug shot atop the message, "This man is wanted for treasonous activities against the United States." The article further claimed President Kennedy was ". . . turning the sovereignty of the U.S. over to the communist controlled United Nations." I didn't consider him a conservative Democrat, not in the southern style, anyway, but he was a long way from being a Communist.

When I returned to the second floor to prepare for surgery, I went into the doctors' lounge. Dr. Baxter, the staff surgeon who was to assist me that morning, was there smoking a cigarette and drinking coffee. Next, I walked down the hall to the anesthesiologist's call-room to speak to the doctor who would be working with us. The television was on, and I noticed that Dallas Police Chief Jesse Curry was on the air. I reached over, turned up the volume, and listened as he admonished the citizens of Dallas to behave themselves and to make the President feel welcome.

7:15 A.M.
Irving, Texas

Lee Harvey Oswald leaves for his recently acquired job at the Texas School Book Depository in downtown Dallas. He is given a ride by coworker Buell Frazier. Oswald has in his possession a 24–27-inch long paper bag, which he places in the backseat of Frazier's car, telling Frazier they are "curtain rods."

Oswald, born in 1939 in New Orleans, had lived in various cities including New York and Fort Worth. As a tenth-grade dropout, he had entered the Marines in 1956. He was trained in radar operations and stationed at a top-secret base for U-2 spy plane operations in the Philippines. He was also schooled, and became proficient, in the Russian language.

In September of 1959, he requested, and was granted, an early hardship discharge in order to take care of his ailing mother. He traveled to his mother's home in Fort Worth, where he remained for three days before leaving for New Orleans. At New Orleans he boarded a ship and journeyed to Russia where he met and married Marina Prusakova. While in Russia, Oswald attempted to renounce his American citizenship, defect, and turn over secret radar information to the Soviets. Soon thereafter, one of America's U-2 spy planes was shot down over Russia, an incident that effectively disrupted the planned summit conference between President Eisenhower and Premier Krushchev.

Oswald, upon returning to the United States with his Russian wife and new daughter in June of 1962, was never questioned by authorities about his attempted defection nor his passing of secret information to our cold-war enemy. That there were no charges of treason brought against Oswald is only one of the many strong indicators of his connection to some agency of this government.

7:55 A.M.

Texas School Book Depository—Dallas

Oswald and Frazier arrive for work. Oswald removes the package of "curtain rods" from the car and carries it with one end in his right hand and the other end in his armpit. It is this package, authorities would later claim, that Oswald used to sneak the alleged murder weapon into the Depository.

8:06 A.M.

Hotel Texas—Fort Worth

President Kennedy and Larry O'Brien, his close friend and aide, look out the hotel window at the parking lot below, where the President will give a speech in a few minutes. Kennedy tells O'Brien, "If someone wanted to get you, it wouldn't be difficult, would it?"

In retrospect, there appears to have been good reason for this observation. The Protective Research Section, a preventive intelligence division of the Secret Service, had received information on more than 400 possible threats to the President during the period from March through November 1963. Approximately 20 percent of these threats could be attributed to political motivation. In 1979, the House Select Committee on Assassinations reviewed computerized summaries of these threats and determined three of them to be significant.

The first was a postcard warning that the President would be assassinated while riding in a motorcade. No other information was given by the committee except to simply say that the card resulted in additional protection being provided when the President went to Chicago in March. We do know, however, that a previous attempt on the President's life in Chicago was foiled on November 5, 1960. The then Senator Kennedy was the Democratic presidential nominee and was campaigning at a giant rally at Chicago Stadium. It was three days before the election. A twenty-three-year-old Puerto Rican, Jaime Cruz Alejandro, was subdued and disarmed by six policemen as he shoved his way toward Kennedy's open convertible with a loaded pistol.

The second significant threat of 1963, as determined by the House Select Committee on Assassinations, again involved Chicago and possibly resulted in the cancellation of the President's planned visit to the city for a parade and to attend the Army–Air Force football game at Chicago Stadium. On October 30, 1963, the Secret Service learned that Chicago resident Thomas Arthur Vallee, an outspoken critic of Kennedy's foreign policy, was in possession of several weapons and had requested time off from his job on November 2, the date of the President's planned visit. Arrested by Chicago police, Vallee was found with an M-1 rifle, a handgun, and 3,000 rounds of ammunition in his automobile. He was released that evening.

More information about Vallee was discovered by the Secret Service prior to the President's trip to Dallas on November 22. The suspect, it was learned, was a Marine Corps veteran with a history of mental illness, a member of the John Birch Society, and a self-styled, expert marksman. None of this information was forwarded to the agents responsible for protecting the President during his trip to Texas. A Secret Service report, however, dated four days *after* the assassination, noted the similarity between the background of Vallee and that of accused assassin Lee Harvey Oswald. Was Vallee the proposed fall guy in a Chicago plot as Oswald was in Dallas?

It now appears there was another plot in Chicago planned for the same day, one that was much more sinister and complex than the "lone-nut" scenario outlined previously.

Abraham Bolden, the first black to serve on the Secret Service's White House detail, has shed some light on this probable assassination attempt. Bolden had been assigned to the Chicago office in 1963. He alleged that shortly before November 2, the FBI notified the Chicago Secret Service office that it had received a teletype message stating that an attempt would be made on the President's life by a four-man team using high-powered rifles. At least one member of the team, Bolden said, had a Spanish-sounding name. Agents assigned to the Chicago Secret Service office were questioned by the House Select Committee on Assassinations in the late 1970s and were unable to document Bolden's allegations. There is, however, no evidence of the committee having questioned the FBI about the existence of such a message.

After the assassination, an urgent report from the acting special agent in charge of the Chicago Secret Service office detailed the receipt of reliable information about "a group in the Chicago area who may have a connection with the JFK assassination." A member of this group, a Cuban exile, Homer S. Echevarria, an outspoken critic of President Kennedy, reportedly stated that his group now had "plenty of money" and would soon be buying more military arms "as soon as we (or they) take care of Kennedy." The financial backers were reported to consist in part of "hoodlum elements" who were "not restricted to Chicago."

Further recognizing the need to investigate Echevarria and his group, the Secret Service discussed their information with the FBI. The FBI responded that Echevarria and his group, though affiliated with some of the more militant anti-Castro terrorists, were not likely to be involved in any illegal acts.

Reluctant to accept the FBI's representation in light of the evidence, the Secret Service prepared to continue its investigation. Their attempts were blocked when the new President, Lyndon Johnson, appointed the Warren Commission and ordered the FBI to assume primary investigative responsibility. The order came down, not only to the Secret Service, but also to the Dallas Police Department, that the FBI would take "full responsibility," not joint responsibility, for the post-assassination investigation of conspiracies. Secret Service Agent Abraham Bolden's information was buried.

The last of the three significant threats occurred on November 9, when an informant for the Miami Police secretly recorded a conversation with a right-wing extremist named Joseph A. Milteer. Milteer outlined an existing plot to assassinate the President with a high-powered rifle from a tall building. The Secret Service was informed of this threat on November 12. A scheduled motorcade for the President's visit to Miami on November 18 was canceled.

It is obvious from the transcription of the secretly recorded conversation that this plot to kill the President was ongoing and flexible. Milteer stated, "It's in the works . . . there ain't any countdown to it. We have just got to be sitting on go. Countdown, they can move in on you—and on go they can't. Countdown is all right for a slow prepared operation. But in an emergency operation, you have got to be sitting on go." Though this statement presented an existing and persistent plot—information that was in the hands of the Secret Service—no effort was made to relay this threat to the agent in charge of preparations for the trip to Texas. (Transcripts of this recording were given to the Warren Commission and are in the National Archives in Washington, D.C.)

In light of the quick arrest of Oswald, an obvious patsy, it appears Milteer's further statement that, "They will pick up somebody . . . within hours afterward . . . just to throw the public off," was not guesswork.

Five days after the Secret Service was informed of the Milteer threat, and only five days before the President's death, another

FBI teletype was reportedly received in the New Orleans FBI office. FBI Security Code Clerk William Walter received the message. It warned of a conspiracy, "to assassinate President Kennedy on his proposed trip to Dallas, Texas, November 22–23, 1963," and that "a militant revolutionary group" were the plotters. Milteer was connected with several radical and militant right-wing organizations and traveled extensively throughout the United States in support of their views.

FBI Agent Walter's charge that the FBI received information of a Dallas plot was denied by Harry Maynard of the New Orleans office.

The failure of government agencies to heed prior warnings of assassination plots against the President's life is well documented. Their inaction, and almost total neglect of precautionary measures, is appalling—if not suspicious. These agencies, however, are not alone in this regard. It appears that Louisiana authorities must share some responsibility for the Dallas assassination. Two days prior to November 22, 1963, they received information that two men were on their way to Dallas to kill the President. Of all the prior warnings of plots on the President's life, perhaps none is more chilling than the one given by former Ruby employee Rose Cheramie.

On November 20, 1963, Cheramie was

found bruised and disoriented, lying beside a road near Eunice, Louisiana. The state trooper who found her reported that, while driving her to the hospital, she described being abandoned by two men whom she perceived to be of Italian extraction. The men, she said, were on their way from Miami to Dallas to kill the President. The trooper described her to be lucid and her account to be quite believable. Several employees of the hospital confirmed that Cheramie had stated before the assassination that the President was going to be murdered.

As bizarre as it may appear, Louisiana State Police *did not* report this revelation to the Secret Service or other officials until *after* the murder of Oswald. Only then was Dallas Police Captain Will Fritz notified of this information. Fritz replied that he was not interested, and Louisiana authorities dropped the matter.

Rose Cheramie was killed on September 4, 1965, one of more than fifty individuals associated with the investigation of the Kennedy assassination who died within three years of that event. Her death, like her allegations concerning two men planning to kill the President, is shrouded in mystery.

Again, she was found injured and lying beside a road, and was taken to a nearby hospital. Her death certificate read DOA (dead on arrival) in three places. Official hospital records, however, describe treatment of her injuries over a period of more than eight hours. Significantly, these records also describe a "deep punctate stellate" wound to her right forehead in addition to other injuries. The wound to Cheramie's forehead as described, according to medical textbooks, occurs in contact gunshot wounds—that is, when a gun barrel is placed against a victim's body and discharged. It is especially applicable to a gunshot wound of the skull in which the thin layer of skin overlying bone traps gases from the weapon and causes expansion between the skin and outer table of the skull, thus lifting up and ballooning the skin and producing tears of a stellate (starlike) or cruciform-appearing wound of entrance.

Unfortunately, the autopsy that could shed light on the cause of Cheramie's death cannot be found by the responsible authorities. Investigation of the alleged "accident" revealed no blood, flesh, or hair on the automobile involved. The driver charged with striking Cheramie swears that he did not hit her. He has also stated that upon stopping to render aid and to transport the victim to medical facilities, he saw a late-model red Chevrolet parked nearby. Cheramie's sister confirms the red Chevy story. She was told by investigating authorities that they too had seen the automobile at the scene shortly before the accident as they made their usual patrol of the area.

Was the death of Rose Cheramie an accident or was it murder? We may never know. In either event, Louisiana authorities failed in their duty to report her warning to those charged with protecting the life of the President.

President Kennedy's philosophical approach to the prevention of his own assassination proved an accurate observation. He had scoffed at many of the measures designed to protect him, and his frequent travel and contact with crowds posed a major problem for the Secret Service. His policies were liberal and sometimes innovative. None of these traits, however, caused his death. That burden of guilt rests squarely on the shoulders of the agencies and officials sworn to law and order and charged with the responsibility of protecting the nation's leader.

Perhaps the Secret Service's negligence is best summarized in the House Select Committee on Assassinations' report which states, "President Kennedy did not receive adequate protection," and that the agency "was deficient in the performance of its duties," and "possessed information that was not properly analyzed, investigated or used . . . in connection with the President's trip to Dallas."

Parkland Hospital—Dallas

I was in the ready room reassuring a very groggy patient that the surgery would go well, and that he would be fine because he had the best surgeons in the country taking care of him. Of course, I wasn't kidding. The self-assurance of a surgeon is mandatory when literally holding a life in his hands—when critical decisions and quick, skilled action are essential. The saying went, "Every surgeon who's worth his salt is stuck for an answer to the question 'who are the three best surgeons in the country?' " The dilemma was coming up with names for the other two.

That morning Dr. Tom Shires was in Galveston, Texas, attending a meeting of the Western Surgical Association. Standing in his place to assist me with the operation was Dr. Charles R. Baxter, a legend in his own time. Dr. Baxter was four years my senior, and had, along with Dr. Shires, greatly influenced my decision to become a surgeon. We were both from Paris, Texas. He had played the role of a big brother to me while we were growing up.

While the junior resident and intern who were to assist me were completing their prep duties, Dr. Baxter and I were at the scrub sink in the hall just outside the operating room, sterilizing our hands while we discussed the research we were conducting at the medical school on regional abdominal hypothermia.

Through ongoing research at Parkland Hospital aimed at reducing the number of deaths from shock due to trauma, we discovered that when chilled Ringer's lactate sluice (salt water) is poured into the exposed abdomen, significant physiological changes rapidly occurred, improving the patient's chances for survival. When four or five liters of Ringer's lactate enter the abdomen, it serves two important functions. First, the core temperature of the kidneys is abruptly reduced, preventing the death of the organs caused by oxygen starvation from reduced blood supply. This avoided acute renal failure, which usually carried a 90 to 100 percent casualty rate. Second, the Ringer's lactate is quickly absorbed through the peritoneum, then passed into the liver where it emerges as plasma look-alike. This is added protection for the patient in hemorrhagic shock when there is substantial blood loss.

As the body goes into hemorrhagic shock, which occurs from an inadequate volume of circulating blood, the vessels constrict and a vacancy we called the third space develops. In such a condition, the body's sodium is lost into the cells. Sodium is necessary to maintain blood pressure and to expand cells for delivery of oxygen to the kidneys and other organs. Under trauma conditions, with significant blood loss, Ringer's lactate supplements this process to minimize the possibility of kidney destruction, which brings on the renal shock. In 1963, there were only two kidney dialysis machines in the city of Dallas, and thus, this medical breakthrough was especially invaluable.

Thanks to the research on Ringer's lactate at Parkland Hospital and Southwestern Medical School, damage to the kidneys during trauma can still be prevented and lives are saved. This same medical technology was implemented throughout the world as standard procedure when treating trauma patients. For this important breakthrough, Drs. Tom Shires and Charles Baxter should have received the first Nobel Prizes at Parkland.

After Dr. Baxter and I had finished scrubbing, we entered the operating room where he loudly sang the Sugar Bear Cereal song he had heard while watching television with his sons. The nurses immediately broke into laughter, and whatever tension may have existed in that room instantly evaporated. It's easy to see why Dr. Baxter was the most loved man at Parkland.

We were wearing shoes with copper brads, and the nurses didn't wear nylon undergarments, precautions taken so that a charge from static electricity or a spark from the floor would not blow up the operating room. We were still using cyclopropane, an explosive type of anesthesia.

As the scrub nurse helped Dr. Baxter into his surgical gloves, he asked her if she had gotten "any" the previous evening, referring to sex, of course. Again, all present broke up in laughter. At that point, Dr. Kenneth Salyer, the junior resident, joined us in the operating room to assist in the surgery. Dr. Salyer had the worst job of all that day, which was to hold the liver back with a toweled retractor while I performed the operation. Believe me, holding that liver for two hours is pure hell.

"Surgical 'B' is now in session," I announced as Pat Schrader, the scrub nurse, handed me a scalpel.

When I made the incision on the patient's right side, just below the ribs, Dr. Baxter remarked that all bleeding ceases in the end, which was a sarcastic implication that the patient might bleed to death in the time it took me to clamp the blood vessels. I never saw anyone do it fast enough to escape Dr. Baxter's vicious tongue.

I had cut through the layers of the muscle and was ready to enter the lining of the abdomen. After verifying that the bowel was not going to be punctured, as can occur when it rests just below this lining, I made a slice with scissors, exposing the abdominal cavity.

9:00 A.M.

Hotel Texas—Fort Worth

President Kennedy returns to the Hotel Texas for the Chamber of Commerce breakfast. As he crosses the street the President chats with Tarrant County Sheriff Lon Evans. Several minutes later Jacqueline arrives with Secret Service agents as the audience cheers.

She is wearing a pink suit with navy lapels and a matching pink pillbox hat. The President looks irritated because her entry receives so much attention.

Meanwhile former Vice President Richard Nixon is at Dallas' Love Field, awaiting his flight out of Dallas. He has been in the city ostensibly to attend a board meeting of the Pepsi-Cola Bottling Company, which his firm represents. He was later to recall that his time in Dallas was November 20–21, 1963, and that he was not there on the day of the President's assassination. He, along with convicted Watergate burglar and CIA agent E. Howard Hunt, are the only two men encountered in subsequent years who do not remember where they were at the time of the assassination.

9:30 A.M.

Dallas

Nightclub owner Jack Ruby arises for the day and proceeds to downtown Dallas. Ruby, born Jacob Rubenstein in Chicago in 1911, had been a runner for mobster Al Capone in the late 1920s. Ruby's mob-related activities continued when he moved to Dallas in 1947. As an antecedent to his move to Dallas, the Chicago mob attempted to bribe the Dallas sheriff and to take over gambling, prostitution, and other vices in Dallas. Ruby was to run these criminal activities and serve as liaison to Chicago's underworld. In 1952, Ruby and two other associates purchased the Bob Wills Ranch House and renamed it the Vegas Club. In 1959, Ruby and another associate purchased a private club in the heart of downtown Dallas. A year later the club was renamed the Carousel Club and began to feature striptease shows. During this same period Ruby also became an informant for the FBI, a fact kept well hidden from the American public for approximately ten years. The Warren Commission denied Ruby's strong organized crime ties despite overwhelming evidence. A later investigation by a Congressional committee confirmed these ties.

Julius Hardie, an employee of a Dallas electrical equipment company, is proceeding east on Commerce Street, nearing Dealey Plaza's triple underpass. As was his custom when in that area, he attempted to get a glimpse of his father-in-law who often worked in the nearby railroad yard. He noticed three men on top of the underpass, two of whom were carrying "long guns." Hardie called the authorities after the assassination and was visited by two FBI agents. He related his story to the two agents but never heard from them again. The FBI has no report of this incident in its files.

10:14 A.M.

Hotel Texas—Fort Worth

President Kennedy and Jackie return to their hotel suite, where the President calls former Vice President John Nance Garner, wishing him a happy ninety-fifth birthday. Moments later, Kennedy is shown the full-page advertisement in the *Dallas Morning News*, which is extremely critical of his administration and attacks him personally.

Parkland Hospital—Dallas

"Keep the goddamn liver out of the way," I barked at the junior resident. Dr. Salyer's hand was already tired from having to apply continuous pressure to the inside of the abdomen. The operation was progressing smoothly, and the patient was stable. As I continued through the procedure, I asked Dr. Baxter, "Are you going to take off early, go downtown, and watch Kennedy's parade?"

Dr. Baxter shook his head and replied that the only way he would see "that son of a bitch" would be if he came to the back door of the hospital. The back of Parkland was the emergency entrance, and Dr. Baxter was the staff surgeon in charge of the emergency room. His reference to the President of the United States wasn't as disrespectful as it might seem, considering Baxter called everyone a son of a bitch. It was the personal pronoun he used for man and objects alike.

Dr. Baxter continued by asking if I thought Jacqueline was as sensuous as she was (and still is) beautiful. My reply was in the Baxter tradition. "If she is, the President is the luckiest son of a bitch in this world."

10:30 A.M.
Dallas

At the office of the Dallas County Sheriff's Department, at the corner of Main and Houston overlooking Dealey Plaza, longtime sheriff Bill Decker meets with his deputies. He instructs them to remain outside the building, but stresses that they are to take absolutely *no* part in the security of the motorcade. Reportedly, these unusual orders had been delivered to Decker via a phone call from a still *unknown* source in the nation's capitol.

10:40 A.M.

Hotel Texas—Fort Worth

President Kennedy's motorcade leaves the Texas Hotel for Carswell Air Force Base in Fort Worth for the short thirteen-minute flight to Dallas.

10:50 A.M.

Dealey Plaza—Dallas

Twenty-three-year-old Julia Ann Mercer, driving west on Elm Street, enters Dealey Plaza, a small parklike area just west of the downtown section of Dallas. She passes the Texas School Book Depository Building while heading toward the triple underpass. In front of her, blocking traffic, is an illegally parked pickup truck in the right lane. The vehicle is stopped with its right wheels on the sidewalk and its left side blocking her lane. While Mercer is behind the truck waiting to pass, she observes a white male wearing a plaid shirt stepping out of the passenger's side and walking around to the truck's side-mounted toolboxes. There he removes what appears to be a rifle wrapped in paper and proceeds to walk up the grassy embankment toward a wooden fence. Finally, upon being able to go around the truck, she looks into the face and locks eyes with its driver.

Later that same day, after the assassination, Mercer gave an affidavit at the Dallas County Sheriff's office where she was interrogated for several hours by uniformed officers, as well as plainclothes personnel whom she believed to be federal investigators.

Early the following morning, FBI agents came to her apartment, requesting that she accompany them back to the sheriff's office. There she was shown approximately a dozen photographs. They requested that she pick out any she recognized as being the men she had seen in the pickup truck. She selected two photographs from the group, but was given no information as to their identity.

On Sunday, the day following her identification, she viewed television coverage of the Oswald shooting. She immediately identified Ruby as the driver of the truck and Oswald as the man with the rifle—the same men she had previously selected from the FBI photographs.

When the subject of Mrs. Mercer's information came up before the Warren Commission, Secret Service Agent Forrest Sorrells testified he decided not to investigate her claim because ". . . this lady said she thought she saw somebody that looked like he had a gun case. But then I didn't pursue that any further because then I had gotten the information that the rifle had been found in the building and shells and so forth."

Parkland Hospital—Dallas

After we had finished suturing the incision and dressing the abdomen, the patient was transported to the recovery room. I smoked a cigarette and drank coffee in the lounge with Dr. Baxter. I then walked down the hall to the recovery room to make sure my patient was still stable and to write postop orders.

11:03 A.M.

Honolulu

Across the Pacific Ocean, six members of the President's cabinet leave Honolulu for

Japan. The prior day, other members of the President's cabinet had been meeting in Honolulu for a nine-hour conference on Vietnam. This group of high-level political and military policymakers had decided to step up military operations against Communist insurgents in this Southeast Asia country. This was in direct conflict with the Presidential decision to reduce U.S. troop strength in the area.

It is highly unusual, if not unheard of, for so many members of the Presidential cabinet to be away from the nation's capitol at a given time.

Parkland Hospital—Dallas

The operation had been completed, and the patient was stable. I was in a good mood because in just a few hours I would be going home. We were closing the abdomen by carefully suturing the muscles in a layered manner as we worked our way to the surface of the belly. With the critical part of the operation completed, Dr. Baxter was ready to get out of there and smoke a cigarette.

During the two hours we had been in surgery, in excess of twenty patients had been treated in the emergency room.

11:40 A.M.

Love Field—Dallas

Dallas Police Chief Jesse Curry meets President Kennedy at Love Field. The President is impressed with the turnout and exclaims, "This doesn't look like an anti-Kennedy crowd."

Five minutes later the limousine leaves Love Field for downtown Dallas. Secret Service Agent William Greer is driving the automobile. Governor John Connally and his wife, Nellie, are in the jump seat. The President and Jacqueline sit together in the rear. Close behind the Presidential limousine is the Secret Service follow-up car carrying ten Secret Service agents. Vice President Lyndon Johnson and Senator Ralph Yarborough are riding together in a convertible to the rear of the Secret Service.

Parkland Hospital—Dallas

After finishing in the recovery room, I stepped back down the hall to get a cup of coffee in the lounge and to thank Dr. Baxter for assisting me with the operation.

12:00 noon
Dallas Morning News Building—Dallas

Reporter Hugh Aynesworth sees Jack Ruby at the Dallas Morning News Building. Ruby later uses the statements of Aynesworth and other employees of the newspaper as confirmation as to his whereabouts during the assassination. Three days after the assassination, however, Aynesworth told the FBI that "Ruby was seen there . . . but was missed for a period of about twenty to twenty-five minutes," and that "he had no information as to where Ruby had gone during this interval of time, nor did other employees. Shortly after Ruby had been missed, people began to come to the office of the newspaper announcing the assassination of President John F. Kennedy, and Ruby appeared shortly thereafter and feigned surprise at this announcement and gave some show of emotion over the news that had been received." Aynesworth also advised that "In view of the fact that the Dallas Morning News Building is removed only about four blocks from the point where the Presidential motorcade passed, I could not understand why if Ruby had a love and devotion to the President as he claims he has, he had not walked this short distance for the purpose of seeing the President pass by."

Dealey Plaza—Dallas

While the motorcade proceeds along its journey to the Trade Mart, suspicious activities continue to occur in Dealey Plaza. Railroad supervisor Lee Bowers, Jr., from his position in a railroad tower behind Dealey Plaza's wooden fence, observes three strange out-of-state cars cruise slowly in and out of his area. Each automobile is driven by a white male, one of whom appears to be talking over a hand-held microphone.

Ed Hoffman, off work for a dental appointment, realizes he is near the parade route and stops his car on Stemmons Freeway west of the Depository, in hopes of seeing the President. From this vantage point he is able to view the area behind the wooden fence. There, he notices two men standing a few feet apart, looking over the fence.

Carolyn Walther, on her lunch break from a nearby dress factory, is standing at a position catty-cornered to the Texas School Book Depository in front of the Dallas County Records Building. She sees two men, one holding a rifle, in the southwesternmost window of the Depository's sixth floor. High-schooler

Arnold Rowland, a few feet south of Walther, also notices the rifleman in that position. Meanwhile, unemployed steelworker Richard Carr is job hunting on the seventh floor of the new courthouse building being constructed at the corner of Houston and Commerce. He, too, notices two men on the sixth floor.

12:15 P.M.

Dealey Plaza—Dallas

It is approximately fifteen minutes prior to the arrival of the motorcade into Dealey Plaza as Jerry Belknap, dressed in army fatigues and standing on the west side of Houston Street, suddenly faints. An ambulance is dispatched to take the twenty-three-year-old part-time newspaper employee to the hospital. Ten minutes later (and five minutes before the shooting), C. L. Bronson sees the arrival of the ambulance to pick up Belknap. From his position, at the corner of Main and Houston, he records this commotion with a home movie camera. In doing so, he also captures what appears to be the movement of two and possibly three people in the

easternmost sixth-floor Depository windows.
Belknap is taken to Parkland Hospital, but
disappears before treatment. His background
is never checked, and Bronson's film is never
analyzed.

Parkland Hospital—Dallas

After hearing another one of Dr. Baxter's over-
ripe jokes, I finished my coffee and walked past
the double doors into the surgical ward. I pulled
some charts, entered the doctors' room next to the
nurses' station, sat down at the desk, and began
writing orders. I remember how upbeat I was as I
wrote out those instructions, knowing all the while
that I had the afternoon and evening free.

12:25 P.M.
Texas School Book Depository

Depository employee Carolyn Arnold sees
Oswald on the first floor near the front door
of the building.

12:29 P.M.

Motorcade—Dallas

Geneva Hine, the only employee in the Depository's second-floor offices, observes the electrical power and telephone system go dead.

The Dallas Police radio system's Channel One, reserved for officers participating in the security of the President, is suddenly immobilized.

President Kennedy's limousine passes the Dallas County Courthouse as the motorcade continues north on Houston Street. All along the street and from the windows of the buildings people cheer and wave to the President. The Texas School Book Depository is just ahead. Nellie Connally turns and remarks to the President, "Mr. Kennedy, you can't say that Dallas doesn't love you."

Of course, not all the citizens of Dallas loved the President, as could be said of any city. But Dallas has received undue condemnation for its perceived role in President Kennedy's death. While Dallas had its radical element, the city itself was incidental in the assassination. The executioners of John Kennedy were determined to eliminate him whether it be in Chicago, Miami, Dallas, or any other location. They were "sitting on go."

12:30 P.M.

Motorcade—Dallas

President Kennedy's limousine turns west onto Elm Street, passing the Texas School Book Depository on the right, and slowly proceeds down the grade leading to Stemmons Expressway. Seconds later, shots ring out. The President clutches his throat. Governor Connally flashes a look of anguish. To the horror of the people standing there, the President's head appears to explode as a bullet rips through his skull. People are running, screaming, and covering their children and loved ones to protect them from the hail of bullets. Jacqueline climbs out onto the back of the limousine to retrieve a piece of her husband's head. Secret Service Agent Clint Hill, who is following closely behind, jumps onto the trunk of the car and pushes her back into her seat as they speed away toward Parkland Hospital.

Pipe-fitter Howard Brennan and fifteen-year-old Amos Euins, from their positions on the south side of Elm Street, see a man fire from the sixth-floor easternmost window of the Depository directly in front of them. S. M. Holland, railroad track and signal supervisor, along with several fellow employees, is standing on the triple underpass overlooking Elm Street. Each sees a puff of smoke from the area of the wooden fence, as does Lee Bowers in the nearby railroad tower. Cheryl McKinnon, a college journalism major planning to write about the President's visit, is standing on the north side of Elm Street, and schoolteacher Jean Hill, positioned opposite her across Elm, each witnessed the smoke from the area of the fence. Ed Hoffman, from his vantage point on Stemmons Freeway, watches a man fire a rifle over the fence toward the approaching motorcade.

Dress manufacturer Abraham Zapruder, from his position atop a low concrete pedestal located on the north side of Elm Street near the wooden fence, records the President's assassination with his home movie camera. He hears shots coming from in back of him. He watches in horror as the President's skull explodes in a shower of blood and brain matter and sees him slammed violently backward and to the left. (Zapruder's filming of this fatal moment was strategic. He recorded for history the President's reaction to the volley of shots that struck him in these few short seconds. Significantly, it shows the President's head and upper body being thrown backward toward the rear of the limousine at a speed estimated at 80 to 100 feet per second. This violent movement is consistent with a shot from the wooden fence to his right front—*not* the Book Depository—to his right rear.)

Nightclub singer Beverly Oliver is standing on the south side of Elm Street across from the wooden fence and films the entire assassination with her 8-millimeter camera. She too observes the puff of smoke from the fence. Unfortunately, this valuable film evidence was confiscated by men identifying themselves as government agents. The film has never surfaced. A film taken from her position would have provided the most comprehensive coverage of the entire assassination, scanning the Texas School Book Depository and the wooden fence, at the precise time of the shots.

In all, 277 of the more than 700 witnesses to the shooting have been identified; 107 of these 277 have given their statements as to the origin of the shots that killed the President. Seventy-five percent, or 77 of the 107, reported that at least one shot came from the President's right front—the area of the wooden fence. Though the Warren Commission stated emphatically that all of the shots were fired from the Depository building, to the President's right rear, the majority of witnesses refute this conclusion.

Building engineer J. C. Price is on the roof of the Terminal Annex Building on the south side of Dealey Plaza. He sees a man run from the area behind the wooden fence. Price stated that the man had something in his right hand and "was running very fast, which gave me the suspicion that he was doing the shooting."

Richard Carr, still on the seventh floor of the new courthouse in the aftermath of the shooting, watches as two men run from behind the Texas School Book Depository. The men enter a waiting station wagon and speed off north on Houston Street. Twenty-year-old James Worrell, Jr., witnesses the assassination from the corner of Elm and Houston and panics as the shooting begins. He quickly races northward, up Houston Street, where he sees a man exit from the back door of the Depository and walk quickly south on Houston.

Meanwhile, teacher Jean Hill, who has just seen the President's head explode a few feet in front of her, notices a man running from the area of the wooden fence. (In her 1964 Warren Commission testimony she would state that the fleeing man looked like Jack Ruby.) She quickly crosses the street in pursuit, but is stopped by a man identifying himself as a Secret Service agent and is told that she can go no farther. Hill is one of several witnesses encountering men producing Secret Service identification in that area.

Several feet west of Jean Hill, mail-service owner Malcolm Summers drops to the ground as the shots ring out. Crossing Elm Street to the area of the wooden fence, he is stopped by a man in a suit with an overcoat over his arm. The man reveals a small automatic weapon under the overcoat and tells Summers, "Don't you'all come up here any further. You could get shot."

Dallas policeman Joe Smith is directing traffic at the intersection of Elm and Houston at the time of the shooting. Believing that the shots came from the area of the wooden fence or overpass, he races past the Depository. He, too, comes face to face with a man who identifies himself as Secret Service. Moments later, Police Sergeant D. V. Harkness, while assisting in sealing off the area, observes several "well-armed" men dressed in suits who tell him they are with the Secret Service.

Though it is quite logical that Secret Service agents would be present in the area of a Presidential appearance, the record firmly establishes that none of the twenty-eight agents present in Dallas that day were ever on foot in Dealey Plaza before, during, or immediately following the shots. All of the agents in the motorcade continued to Parkland Hospital and only one returned to the area later in the afternoon.

Parkland Hospital—Dallas

As I ordered additional lab tests for a patient with postop complications, a nurse passing by stopped and spoke to me. I returned her greeting, and she disappeared around the door as she continued on her mission.

12:31 P.M.

Dealey Plaza—Dallas

Still on Stemmons Freeway, Ed Hoffman continues to watch as the rifleman behind the wooden fence runs westward, passes the weapon to another man, then turns, walks calmly in the opposite direction, and disappears. The man taking the weapon quickly breaks it down, places it in a case, and proceeds slowly northward along the railroad tracks. He, too, disappears.

Sergeant Tom Tilson, an off-duty Dallas policeman, and his daughter are in his car just west of the triple underpass. It is a few minutes after the shooting. They watch as a man in dark clothing comes down the railroad embankment to a black automobile. He throws something into the backseat, hurries around to the front, gets into the car, and speeds off westward. Thinking this suspicious, they pursue the vehicle but lose it in the traffic. The man, Tilson later says, looked and dressed like Jack Ruby.

12:32 P.M.

Texas School Book Depository

Building superintendent Roy Truly and policeman M. L. Baker race into the Depository immediately following the shots. They encounter Oswald in the second-floor lunchroom drinking a Coke. It has been approximately ninety seconds since the last shot was fired. Oswald appears calm and unafraid. Later the Warren Commission is to conclude, rather illogically, that this is the man, who, after just having killed one of the world's most powerful men, now hides the weapon, races down four flights of stairs, pops a soft drink, then casually greets a police officer—not even out of breath—all in ninety seconds.

12:33 P.M.

Washington, D.C.

A breakdown in the telephone system in the nation's capital occurs. It will not be restored for almost an hour.

A short time later, aboard the military aircraft carrying six members of the President's cabinet to Japan, a teletype message reports that shots have been fired at the President. With specific procedures for such an emergency, officials attempted to reach the White House Situation Room. They were prevented from doing so because the official code book was missing from its special place aboard the plane.

12:37 P.M.

Parkland Hospital—Dallas

The telephone rings at Parkland's emergency room nurses' station. The Dallas Police Department advises Doris Nelson, head nurse in emergency, that President Kennedy has been shot and is en route to the hospital. Nelson immediately orders personnel to prepare Trauma Room 1 for the President's arrival.

12:38 P.M.

Parkland Hospital—Dallas

I had just completed writing instructions on the first chart when I heard the unbelievable over the public address system. "Paging Dr. Tom Shires. Paging Dr. Tom Shires," the voice urgently uttered. I couldn't have been more shocked. I simply couldn't believe I had heard it.

Two things never happened at Parkland—face-lift surgery and the chief of surgery being paged over the intercom. If someone needed Dr. Shires, a messenger was sent. Hearing Dr. Shires' name echoing from the ceiling speaker scared me. I was concerned that one of the patients Dr. Shires had entrusted to me in his absence was experiencing upper gastrointestinal hemorrhaging. I immediately picked up the telephone and dialed "O" to answer the page.

"Mert, this is Dr. Crenshaw. Dr. Shires is out of town. What do you need?"

"Dr. Crenshaw, the President has been shot!"

After a moment of intense silence, I replied, "If you're kidding me, I'll kill you."

"This is no joke, Dr. Crenshaw."

Mert was a buxom woman in her fifties who liked to play practical jokes. But the panic in her voice told me she was serious.

A bone-chilling sensation rushed through my body as I thought of going down to emergency and treating the President of the United States. At that instant any lingering question of why I had become a surgeon was answered definitively once and for all.

I slammed down the phone, jumped from my chair, and bolted through the double doors into the surgical area toward the stairwell leading to the emergency room two floors below us. Dr. Robert McClelland was standing in the hall, perusing the surgical scheduling board located directly across the hall from the doctors' lounge. When he looked up and saw me approaching in a full gallop, a perplexed expression covered his face.

"Bob!" I exclaimed as I came charging up to where he was standing. "The President's been shot; you've got to come with me."

When Bob heard those words, his expression changed to one of astonishment. Without breaking

stride, I grabbed him around the waist and pro-
pelled him along until he was running with me. We
sprinted past the operating rooms, through the anesthesia conference room, and through the doors
into the stairwell. Dr. Ken Salyer, who had sensed
the urgency of the moment by our unusual behavior, followed us down to the emergency room. He
later told me that was the only time in his life that
he had seen either Dr. McClelland or me run
anywhere.

Two Secret Service agents burst through the
swinging doors into the emergency room and
asked for gurneys for the President and Governor
Connally. Dr. Bill Midgett, a second-year ob-gyn
resident, who had delivered Marina Oswald's baby
on October 20, 1963, only about a month earlier
and two days before Lee Harvey Oswald's birthday, was the first doctor to encounter the President
outside the emergency room. Several moments
later, Dr. Midgett and several nurses rolled the
President into Trauma Room 1 with Jacqueline
walking at his side. The President was logged into
the register as patient No. 24740 at 12:38 P.M. Governor Connally was logged in as patient No. 24743,
an indication that other patients were being admitted and treated in the emergency room during the
time when the President was being wheeled in.

As I leaped down the stairs, Dr. McClelland at
my side, I had a terrible fear that I would be the
only resident doctor in the room. I didn't know it,
but Bob had a similar thought, fearing that he
would be the only staff doctor there.

With labored breath Dr. McClelland asked me

what had happened. I remember hearing the coins jingling in his pocket with each step.

"I don't know. I took Shires' page, and Mert told me that Kennedy had been shot."

Once we reached the bottom of the stairwell, we opened the door and rushed into the emergency room. There is always commotion around trauma, but what I saw was sheer bedlam. As we flew by the nurses' station, I yelled, "Which room?" A nurse with tears streaming down her face raised one finger.

I looked to my left and saw a man in a suit running. To my amazement, another man in a suit jumped in his path and smashed a Thompson submachine gun across his chest and face. The first man's eyes immediately turned glassy, and he fell against a gray tile wall, and slithered to the floor unconscious. When I heard that gun slam against his face, I just knew the man's jaw was broken. Normally, I would have rushed over and treated the poor guy, but the President of the United States was waiting for me, and his condition was worse than broken bones. I was to learn later that the man with the gun was a Secret Service agent, and the one who had been hit was an FBI agent. It was a goddamn madhouse in the emergency room . . . people running, yelling. Everyone suspected everyone else—complete and utter paranoia—that's the only way to describe it.

As I turned to continue toward Trauma Room 1, there was Lyndon Johnson, being ushered into one of the minor-medicine cubicles, which were located past the nurses' station and partitioned by sliding curtains. His face was ashen, and he was holding his chest. Only recently, he had had a coronary, and I was afraid he was having another heart attack. Behind the Vice President was Ralph Yarborough, crying.

12:40 P.M.
Dealey Plaza—Dallas

Back in Dealey Plaza, Patrolman J. W. Foster leaves his station atop the triple underpass and moves to the area behind the wooden fence. There he discovers footprints and cigarette butts near the spot where witnesses observed the puff of smoke during the shooting. Continuing around the fence to Elm Street, Foster crosses the thoroughfare to a manhole where witnesses have gathered and where the ground has been disrupted. He is joined by Deputy Sheriff E. R. Walthers and an unidentified man wearing a suit and carrying an overcoat on his arm. The man is later identified by Dallas Police Chief Jesse Curry as an FBI agent but refused to reveal his name. As Foster squats near the manhole and points to the open southwesternmost sixth-floor window of the Book Depository, the "FBI agent" reaches down to the disrupted ground area and retrieves a spent bullet. Standing and turning, the "agent" places the bullet in his pants pocket, and moves away, disappearing into the crowd. This "agent" has never been identified and the bullet never seen again.

Parkland Hospital—Dallas

Moments later, Bob and I entered Trauma Room 1. The first person I came face to face with was Jacqueline Kennedy, who was standing just inside the door in pensive quietness, clutching her purse, her pillbox hat slightly askew. She turned and gazed at me, then refocused her attention on her husband. The look on her face forever marked my memory. Anger, disbelief, despair, and resignation were all present in her expression. I whispered, "My God, my God, it's true."

In 1963, President Kennedy and Jaqueline received the same kind of attention that Prince Charles and Lady Di do today. I had read stories in newspapers and magazines that claimed the President and the First Lady no longer cared for one another, that the perpetuation of their marriage was a necessity because of the Presidency. Human tragedy strips away the facade, exposing the person's core of true feelings and emotions. In all the sentiments I have seen displayed and heard expressed in my thirty years of practice by people grieving and hurting over trauma victims, I never saw or sensed more intense and genuine love than Jacqueline showed at that moment toward her dying husband.

Drying blood caked the right side of Jacqueline's dress and her leg. Her once-white gloves were stained almost completely crimson. If she hadn't been standing, I would have thought she had been shot, too.

As Dr. McClelland and I approached, Dr. Malcom Perry, the assistant professor of surgery, blurted that he and Dr. Jim Carrico, the physician who had first entered the room, had already inserted an endotracheal tube (breathing tube) down the President's throat.

In astonishment, I beheld the President of the United States lying before me. Blood was caked on his steel-gray suit, and his shirt was the same crimson color. Even in that condition, his charisma filled the room. He was a larger man than I had imagined him. In fact, he filled the entire gurney. For someone who had been sickly most of his life, the President looked strong and substantial, just what you expect in a man who had achieved that degree of success.

I was standing at about the President's waist, making a quick inspection of his general appearance. His face was unmarked and exquisite. His eyes were open and divergent. They were still and devoid of life. I immediately became pessimistic.

Then I noticed that the entire right hemisphere of his brain was missing, beginning at his hairline and extending all the way behind his right ear.

Pieces of skull that hadn't been blown away were hanging by blood-matted hair. Based upon my experience with trauma to the head from gunshots, I knew that only a high-velocity bullet from a rifle could dissect a cranium that way. Part of his brain, the cerebellum, was dangling from the back of his head by a single strand of tissue, looking like a piece of dark gray, blood-soaked sponge that would easily fit in the palm of a hand.

Blood was still seeping from the wound onto the gurney, dripping into the kick bucket on the floor. Seeing that, I became even more pessimistic. I also identified a small opening about the diameter of a pencil at the midline of his throat to be an entry bullet hole. There was no doubt in my mind about that wound. I had seen dozens of them in the emergency room. At that point, I knew that he had been shot at least twice.

Other doctors were rushing in to help. Drs. Baxter and Paul Peters, assistant professor of urology, had come from the medical school, and Dr. Salyer had followed us from the second floor. Instinctively, I took the right leg. Dr. Salyer was stationed at my side to assist me. Everyone, physicians and nurses alike, knew what to do, because we had been through this procedure hundreds, if not thousands, of times. But I believed, as I think every doctor in Trauma Room 1 thought, that the President was dead from the very beginning. But goddammit, he was the President of the United States, and we had to do something. After all, we were surgeons.

Drs. McClelland and Ron Jones were stationed at the left arm and chest; Drs. Baxter and Peters took the right side of his torso. With a distressed look on his face, Dr. Baxter glanced at me and shook his head in amazement. There was no doubt in my mind that he was referring to his earlier comment about meeting the President at the back of the hospital.

Turning to my right, I noticed that Jacqueline was still standing in the room. I wasn't sure if there was anything we could do to save her husband, but I didn't want her to witness what we were about to do to him. "Mrs. Kennedy, I think you should step outside," Dr. Baxter said. Without taking her eyes off the President, she turned and walked from the room, watching him until she disappeared through the door. I was relieved.

As I turned back to the President, I spotted another problem. Clint Hill, the Secret Service agent who had pushed Jacqueline back into the car, was rambling around the room in a wild-eyed, disoriented fashion, waving a cocked and ready-to-fire .38 caliber pistol. There we were, getting ready to work on a man who had just lost half his head from a bullet, and we had a crazed man running around with a loaded gun. I didn't know what he was going to do.

Hill had failed to do his job, which was to protect the President of the United States. My concern at that moment was that he would prevent us from doing our jobs, which was to give the President whatever chance we could.

"Baxter," I said as the nurses rushed to wheel into place the portable tables that contained cut-down and chest-tube trays, "what are we going to do about him?'' Before Dr. Baxter could say anything, nurse Doris Nelson, supervisor of the emergency room, a heavyset, granite-faced, nononsense woman, turned to Hill and snapped, "Whoever shot the President is not in this room." Hill didn't respond. "Look," she persisted, "he's okay, he's okay, he's okay," she repeated as she pointed to each doctor. "Now, put away the gun so that we can get to work."

Hill simply vanished. I don't remember seeing him again. Years later, I was informed that he had to be institutionalized because of a nervous breakdown. Hill's behavior in Trauma Room 1 told me that he had already flipped out. Reports were that as the President's limousine sped away from downtown Dallas, he was ferociously beating his fist against the trunk of the car in anguish over the assassination.

While Nelson had been talking to Hill, I removed the President's shoes and right sock, and began cutting off his suit trousers, with nurses Diana Bowron and Margaret Hinchcliffe assisting. Don Curtis, an oral surgery resident, was doing the same thing to the left limb. I noticed that one of the oxfords that I had tossed to the side of the room had a lift in the sole. The President's right leg was three-quarters of an inch longer than his left leg.

After we had cut away his suit pants, we unstrapped his back brace and slung it to the wall and out of the way. When the brace landed on the floor, it remained upright on its side. During World War II, the President had injured his back in a PT-boat accident, requiring the steel harness that became a permanent part of his attire. Articles of clothing were flying throughout the room as we disrobed him. His coat and shirt were simultaneously cut away.

Usually, trauma victims are stripped of all clothing so that an injury will not be overlooked. But no one ever attempted to remove the President's briefs. I think it was out of respect for the man, the dignified position he held, and the principles for which he stood that we subconsciously didn't want him lying there naked. In addition, with the horrendous head wound he had sustained, we weren't concerned with the lower part of his body. If we could have stabilized him, there would have been plenty of time to check for additional injuries.

The President's skin had a bronze cast to it. At first glance he appeared to have a golden tan. But his coloring was not sun related. Rather, it was a physiological phenomenon. Dr. Carrico remembered reading that the President had Addison's disease, because he had had tuberculosis of the adrenal glands. Under such a condition, the skin develops a dark tint. For this problem the President took steroids to compensate for the hormones the glands failed to manufacture. Admiral George Burkley, Kennedy's personal physician, traveling with the Presidential party, gave Dr. Carrico three 100-mg vials of Solu-Cortef from the President's bag.

Today, it is hard to fathom that as recently as 1963, the President of the United States could be brought to a trauma hospital and the attending physicians would not have the benefit of knowing prior to his arrival his blood type or medical history. That was exactly the situation when President Kennedy was wheeled into Parkland. As a matter of policy, the government did not furnish such information to anyone. One of the President's Secret Service agents, Roy Kellerman, informed a nurse that President Kennedy's blood type was O, RH positive.

After the Kennedy assassination, the procedure changed drastically. Now, when a President travels, a designated hospital in the city where he is visiting must maintain fully equipped emergency and operating rooms with trauma and surgical teams ready to go. In addition, the President's complete history is kept in the hospital's computers so that all necessary information is ready for immediate use. During the 1970s, when President Ford was in Fort Worth, I was advised by the government that John Peter Smith Hospital was to be on alert as the designated trauma hospital. The procedures we followed would have given us every conceivable advantage to take care of the President had there been an emergency.

After we had removed the President's clothing, we were ready to begin the ABC's of trauma care—A is airway, B is breathing, C is circulation. I placed my hand on the femoral artery located at his groin. "He may have a pulse," I announced as I felt a possible movement of the artery. "No blood pressure," said a nurse who was monitoring the President's vital signs. "I think I've got a heartbeat here," someone else said. Except for an occasional observation or instruction, there wasn't much talking in Trauma Room 1. Everyone was in awe of the President, and the eminence of his position had a silencing effect upon us all.

Kennedy was barely breathing. The bullet that entered his neck had pierced the windpipe. Dr. Carrico had forced an endotracheal tube down his throat.

While Dr. Carrico had been performing this procedure, three cutdowns (insertion of a plastic tube in the vein to give rapid infusion of fluids intravenously), one arm and both legs, were to start Ringer's lactate because of blood loss (hemorrhagic shock). Dr. Salyer was assisting me with the cutdown on the right leg, and Dr. Curtis began the same surgery on the left limb.

Depending upon the condition of the patient and the severity of his wounds, blood and Ringer's lactate are administered through an IV by sticking a needle into the vessel without doing cutdowns. But when massive amounts of these fluids are needed, an eighteen-gauge catheter (about the size of a pencil lead) is surgically placed directly into the vein by a cutdown procedure in that area.

After I had put on surgical gloves, a sterile sheet with a small window hole was spread over the area that had been prepped, which was on the inside of the President's leg, about two inches above his ankle. I was handed a scalpel, and I made a small incision to expose the saphenous vein. I then clamped off the blood flow and ligated the vessel leading to the foot. After making a small nick in the saphenous vein, I inserted a catheter toward the heart, then tied the space between the vessel and the catheter to prevent leakage. I plugged the IV into the flange of the catheter, the clamp was removed, and Ringer's lactate began flowing. During this ten-minute period, cutdowns had been completed on one arm and two legs, and fluids were moving through the President's body.

When we saw blood frothing around the President's neck wound, it became clear that the endotracheal tube had failed to increase the air volume in his lungs. Dr. Perry decided to perform a tracheostomy on the President's throat, where the bullet had entered his neck, between the second and third tracheal cartilages. After Dr. Perry made a small incision, Drs. McClelland and Baxter helped ease in the tube. The procedure requires more than one person, because the endotracheal tube must be lifted slightly to allow the other tube to slide down the throat.

Moments later, Drs. Baxter and Peters began inserting an anterior chest tube on the President's right side, and Drs. Jones and McClelland were doing the same thing on the left side to further assist in his breathing by expanding his chest cavity.

The doctors inserted the chest tubes into the President's body by making incisions between the ribs on both sides of his chest in the mid-clavicular lines, which are located at the shoulder blade level. Trocars, which are blunt, oblong instruments surrounded by metal tubes, were then plunged through the incisions into his chest cavity. The trocars were then pulled out, and latex rubber tubing with holes in the sides to allow air to pass were fed down through the metal sheaths into the chest cavity. The other ends of the rubber tubing were put into water-sealed drainage to create negative pressure to expand the lungs.

It had been almost twenty minutes since the President had been brought in. A tracheostomy had been performed, and he was on an automatic breathing machine (anesthesia machine); the endotracheal tube, which had been placed down his throat by Dr. Carrico, had been removed after the tracheostomy; and two anterior chest tubes had been inserted to get air to his lungs so that oxygen would be available for his organs, especially his kidneys and brain (or what was left of it). And to transport the oxygen to the President's brain and organs, we had improved his circulation by making the three cutdowns. We had fluids, "O" negative blood and Ringer's lactate flowing into one arm and both legs through the enlarged portals. The ABC's of trauma care had been completed.

I walked to the President's head to get a closer look. His entire right cerebral hemisphere appeared to be gone. It looked like a crater—an empty cavity. All I could see there was mangled, bloody tissue. From the damage I saw, there was no doubt in my mind that the bullet had entered his head through the front, and as it surgically passed through his cranium, the missile obliterated part of the temporal and all the parietal and occipital lobes before it lacerated the cerebellum. The wound resembled a deep furrow in a freshly plowed field. Several years later when I viewed slow-motion films of the bullet striking the President, the physics of the head being thrown back provided final and complete confirmation of a frontal entry by the bullet to the cranium.

When I saw the severity of the head wound, I

thought that everything we had done for him during those twenty minutes was a complete waste of time. It was a four-plus injury, which no one survives. (In emergency medicine, injuries are described as one-plus, two-plus, etc. A four-plus injury is a worst-case scenario.) Correspondingly, we made a four-plus effort to change that statistic. If President Kennedy had, in some miraculous way, survived the attack, he would have remained in a perpetual vegetative state. Never again would he have uttered another sound or opened his eyes.

Dr. Kemp "High Pockets" Clark, a six-foot six-inch-tall neurosurgeon and associate professor and chairman of the Neurosurgery Division, entered the room, put on a pair of rubber gloves, and examined the President's cranium. I remember Dr. Clark frowning while shaking his head in despair as he looked on.

"Kemp, tell us how bad that head injury is," Dr. Baxter said, "because we are losing him."

"My God, the whole right side of his head is shot off," Dr. Clark replied. "We've got nothing to work with."

Dr. M. T. "Pepper" Jenkins, professor and chairman of the Anesthesia Department, and other anesthesiologists hooked up a torpedo (a machine that measures heartbeats) to the President. When it was switched on, the green light moved across the screen in a straight line, without a hint of even the slightest cardiac activity. Dr. Clark noted that the President's eyes were fixed and dilated. Glancing at us, Dr. Clark again shook his head, indicating that it was too late.

Dr. Perry, bless his heart, just wouldn't give up. He began closed-chest cardiac massage on the President, while Dr. Pepper Jenkins continued to administer pure oxygen. None of us wanted to quit. When Dr. Perry's hands got tired, Dr. Clark took over. But in a few moments, it became clear that absolutely nothing could be done to save the man, and all efforts ceased. Dr. Fouad A. Bashour, associate professor of internal medicine, quickly connected a cardiotachy scope, which was a more sensitive machine than the torpedo, to the President. Again, the straight green light traversed the scope. Jenkins reached over and closed the valve to the anesthesia machine. We had just witnessed the most tragic event imaginable, the President's death.

As I panned the room, it took on a coldness, an ugliness it never had before. The gray wall tiles looked impersonal, almost offensive. Against the somberness of the black rubber floor, bloody gauze and bandages, empty bottles, boxes, paper, pieces of tubing, and the President's clothing were strewn everywhere. The artifacts of pain and death underscored the darkness of the moment, the sorrow within our hearts. Forever lodged in my memory was the dispassionate visage of that chamber.

Having minored in history and being a Civil War buff, I couldn't help thinking of Abraham Lincoln, another President brutally killed, shot in the head. Suddenly, I identified with the helpless feeling Lincoln's physician had surely experienced. I felt sorry for him, because I was feeling sorry for myself and for everyone else in the room.

I later considered other bizarre similarities in the deaths of the two Presidents. Among many, both had Vice Presidents named Johnson and both were slain in the presence of their wives.

Down the hall, doctors had just rescued a man who had been injured when he drove his truck into a concrete pillar. We could help a drunk, but we couldn't save the President of the United States. I felt cheated, because we never had a chance to use on the President the medical technology that was developed at Parkland to save trauma victims. The only thing that would have saved John F. Kennedy that day was a quick-acting Secret Service agent or a bullet-proof bubble on his limousine. Even with the medical advancements of the last twenty-eight years, there is still nothing that can save a victim who loses the entire right side of his brain. The combined hemorrhagic shock and loss of neurologic functions are too great to overcome.

From a humanitarian standpoint, it shouldn't have made any difference whether it was the drunk or the President lying there. We always give an all-out effort, because as Dr. Baxter so insightfully put it, "A life is a life is a life." But that man on the gurney was different. He wasn't just another trauma victim. He was the President of the United States of America.

My perceptions of my country and its principles were forever altered that day. We all proceed through life with a degree of bravado, especially those of us in medicine. But I never believed I would feel fear and vulnerability like I did at that moment. Surgeons are not supposed to get caught up in the emotions of death, but this one gave me the chills. I was gazing at a corpse that to me represented the Constitution, the Bill of Rights, and every other democratic tenet that has descended to us through hundreds of years of human genius, effort, and sacrifice. And I was frightened at the thought of someone trying to deny that magnificent heritage with a bullet.

The room was in dead silence, except for the muffled sounds of weeping. Then I looked down into that kick bucket, and I nearly lost my control. There, mingled with the President's brain tissue and his life's blood, were Jacqueline's red roses. Tears welled up in my eyes, and a lump the size of a baseball seized my throat. To me, the contents of that can represented our country—broken, bloody, and hurting. It symbolized the beauty of Nature against the destruction caused by a madman or madmen. It showed what was left of a Presidency, a marriage, and a family, the memory of his two children. Never had the stench of murder filled my nostrils as strongly as it did at that moment.

As I stood there looking at the man, blood still oozing from his head, I wasn't a Democrat; I wasn't a Republican; I wasn't a Liberal; I wasn't a Conservative. I was an American, who had just lost my President. Sure, I had been caught up in regional cynicism, that relic of pride manifesting in North vs. South, Rebel vs. Yankee, us vs. them, which is ingrained into us from childhood as part of our culture. But there's a plateau of decency that rises above all of that, and nothing evokes quicker change in one's perceptions than a tragedy. Suddenly, the scope of our lives was bigger than Texas, the Southwest, or the nation.

We had discovered, as I believe most people do, that witnessing history being made can be almost as unpleasant an experience as making it. I took a deep breath and let it out slowly. I don't remember who shut the President's eyes, but when I helped Dr. Baxter cover the President's body with a sheet, they were closed. It was over. I looked at my wrist-watch—it was 12:52 P.M.

12:52 P.M.

Dallas

The news of the President's death has not yet been announced. But someone in Dallas knows that the job has been done. An emergency telephone call is made from a Riverside 8 exchange to a Pablo Brenner or Bruner in Mexico City. The caller states, "He's dead, he's dead." Obviously the operational capacity of "sitting on go" had become "go"—mission accomplished.

12:55 P.M.

Garland, Texas

In the Dallas suburb of Garland, the phone rings in the court of Dallas County Justice of the Peace Theron Ward. The judge's secretary is still out to lunch, so he answers the call himself. On the other end of the line the excited voice of a Parkland Hospital nurse expresses her relief at being able to reach him. "The President has been shot," she says. "Could you come to the hospital as soon as possible?" The judge immediately dismisses court and hurriedly proceeds by automobile, red lights blinking and siren screaming, to the hospital.

In Texas, it is the duty of a justice of the peace to hold inquests, with or without a jury, in all cases of unlawful death. Because the murder of a President was not a federal crime in 1963, responsibility for its investigation and prosecution legally belonged to officials of the state of Texas. How this responsibility was usurped by the federal government has become one of the major questions in official rulings concerning the President's death.

The thirty-nine-year-old Judge Ward, a man with a ninth-grade education, was a Navy veteran of World War II in the South Pacific. Shot nine times, he carried a steel plate in his head. Following the war, he served five years as a Dallas deputy sheriff and five years with the Dallas police. Having been only recently elected as justice of the peace, and with minimal legal background, the judge is about to be forced to make one of the most controversial and critical decisions in the aftermath of the President's assassination.

Parkland Hospital—Dallas

During the twenty minutes we had been working on the President, everyone in the emergency room remained in utter bewilderment. In the confusion, FBI and Secret Service agents, as well as the Dallas police, were rushing around, trying to identify one another and secure the hospital. News reporters were trying to get the story, and the medical personnel were endeavoring to process other patients in the midst of mania. Parkland's switchboard was shut down to most incoming calls so that all available telephone lines could be used by the authorities. Other injured patients arriving at the emergency room continued to filter through the mayhem for treatment. Through the thick of it all, the hospital managed to care for the public, as was the Parkland way.

When Jacqueline Kennedy wasn't standing outside Trauma Room 1, peeking in to get a glimpse of what was happening each time the door opened, she was at the nurses' station talking by phone to Robert Kennedy and other family members. She had also asked that a priest be sent to the hospital. Drs. James "Red" Duke and David Mebane were stabilizing Governor Connally in Trauma Room 2 by inserting a chest tube and starting intravenous infusion of Ringer's lactate before taking him to x-ray and surgery. Under heavy guard, Lyndon Johnson remained hidden behind a curtain in the minor medicine room just across the hall from the President.

Once the sheet had been placed over the President, it was almost as if all fifteen doctors didn't want to be there. Dr. Baxter and I walked out of the room, and there, to our right, was Jacqueline with an aide standing beside her. When she looked at me, then at Dr. Baxter, she detected in our faces that the President was gone. Words to that effect were not exchanged. Her head tilted downward with saddened eyes fixed on a world without her husband. I placed my arm around her shoulders. So broad were they, that I didn't think my hand would ever reach her arm. I asked her if she would like to lie down in the residents' lounge, which was at the end of the hall next to Trauma Rooms 3 and 4. Back then we didn't have Valium, so I offered her a phenobarbital tablet. She hesitated, then said that she wanted to remain there, just outside Trauma Room 1. Although she looked very composed, I believed she was still in shock, which was understandable. She sat down in a chair and asked a passing aide for a cigarette.

I glanced down at the purse she was still holding, and noticed that some of the President's brain tissue had not been removed. In a subtle manner, I motioned for the aide to step aside. When he did, I asked him to clean the purse. I looked at my wristwatch. It was 12:55. Out of the corner of my eye I saw a priest walk up and stop by the nurses' station. I stepped back into Trauma Room 1 to make sure everything was ready for the ceremony. One of the several doctors and nurses still in the room was Fouad A. Bashour, our chief of cardiology. He was Catholic, and he understood the significance of giving last rites to the President before he was officially pronounced dead, which had not yet occurred. With everything in order, I opened the door to the room and stepped aside. All of the President's clothes had been neatly folded and placed at one end of the room. I again looked at my wristwatch. It was 12:57 P.M.

1:02 P.M.

Oak Cliff Section of Dallas

Housekeeper Earlene Roberts watches as Lee Harvey Oswald enters the rooming house at 1026 North Beckley and goes to his room. While Oswald is in his room, Roberts hears a car honk outside—two quick short blasts.

She peers out the front window and observes two officers in a Dallas police car drive slowly away. Oswald then emerges from his room and leaves the house. He is last seen by the housekeeper, standing at the bus stop a short distance away.

1:05 P.M.
South of Dallas

A few miles south of Dallas, on Interstate 45, Texas Highway patrolmen stop a black automobile for speeding. Witnesses to the incident observe at least three men in suits in the car. One of the three men identifies himself to the officer as a Secret Service agent and states, "We're in a hurry to get to New Orleans to investigate part of the shooting." However, there is no record of Secret Service personnel being dispatched to New Orleans on the day of the assassination.

Parkland Hospital—Dallas

Father Huber entered the room. Jacqueline Kennedy followed. She stopped at the foot of the gurney. With the exception of his feet, which were exposed, the President's body was covered with a sheet. Dr. Baxter and several other doctors also entered the room. Mrs. Kennedy knelt down and kissed his great (big) toe. Stepping to the head of the cart, Father Huber carefully uncovered the President's head so as not to display the wound. Jacqueline approached, took the President's right hand, and pressed it to her cheek. At this point I was blinking back tears and trying to swallow the lump in my throat. The priest began intoning the last rites.

"John Fitzgerald Kennedy, if you are living, I absolve you from your sins in the name of the Father, the Son, and the Holy Spirit."

As he continued, Jacqueline took off her wedding ring, placed it on the President's little finger, and kissed him on his cheek. And that was when I could stand no more. Tears spilled from my eyes and trickled down my face. The baseball in my throat had turned into a basketball, and I was not alone in that feeling.

As Father Huber dipped his thumb into the holy oil and tracked a cross on the President's forehead, he said, "Through this holy anointing may God forgive you whatever sins you have committed. By the faculty given to me by the Apostolic See, I grant to you a plenary indulgence and remission of all your sins, and I bless you in the name of the Father, and the Son, and the Holy Spirit, Amen." I again looked at my wristwatch. It was 1:01 P.M.

When the priest concluded, Jacqueline left the room. Everyone else followed, except for several nurses, who immediately began preparing President Kennedy to be moved. I joined Drs. Baxter, Perry, Jenkins, and Clark, who had congregated by the nurses' station. They were deciding upon the time of death to be posted on the death certificate that still had to be signed. Although it was 1:10 P.M., the document would show 1:00 P.M. as the time of death, because the administering of the last rites had begun just prior to that moment.

Normally, the job of signing the death certificate was relegated to the least ranking physician on the trauma team, because staff doctors didn't want to be involved in it. In this case that would have been Salyer or Carrico. But for the President of the United States, everyone thought it appropriate that Dr. Clark sign the certificate, because President Kennedy had died of a neurological wound.

Once Dr. Clark had officially recorded the death of the thirty-fifth President, the doctors rushed to Trauma Room 2 to help with Governor Connally. I stayed in Trauma Room 1, because when there is a death, one of the duties of a resident on the trauma team is to make arrangements to process the body, especially if a crime is involved. Under Texas law, a homicide automatically requires an autopsy.

I opened the door to Trauma Room 1 and stuck my head in to check on the progress of the nurses who were preparing the President's body to be transported. When I turned around, I saw, in a group of people whom I believed to be Presidential aides and Secret Service agents, Vernon Stembridge, chief of surgical pathology, and Sidney

Stewart, resident in pathology. The doctors were explaining, politely but forcefully that, pursuant to Texas law, they would be performing an autopsy on President Kennedy's body before it was taken from the hospital. In tones of equal forcefulness, but with greater determination, the men in suits responded that they had orders to take the President's body back to Washington, D.C., just as soon as it was ready to be moved, that there would be no Texas autopsy.

As both sides became more entrenched in their positions, talking turned to shouting and hand waving escalated to finger pointing. Unable to prevail in their mission, Drs. Stembridge and Stewart angrily turned and stomped out of the room. Not only were they outnumbered, but the men in suits had guns. My impression was that someone, who had given explicit instructions to these men, wanted Kennedy's body out of Parkland, out of Dallas, and out of Texas in a hurry. I also thought it unusual to hear Stembridge raising his voice, because he was a quiet, mannerly man.

I again checked on the progress being made on the President's body, then briefly stopped in Trauma Room 2, hoping that a death certificate wouldn't have to be signed for Governor Connally, too.

Since the assassin's bullet had passed through his body, puncturing his right lung, shattering his wrist, and lodging in his thigh, Governor Connally was experiencing difficulty in his breathing and was losing blood. To stabilize the governor, Drs. Duke and Mebane had started an intravenous injection of Ringer's lactate and placed a tube in his right chest to prevent his lung from collapsing. Just after I arrived there, the doctors and nurses were preparing to take the governor to x-ray, before heading to surgery.

1:15 P.M.
Oak Cliff Section of Dallas

At the corner of Tenth and Patton, nine-tenths of a mile from Oswald's rooming house, Dallas Police Officer J. D. Tippit is shot and killed beside his patrol car. Eye-witnesses at the scene give conflicting accounts of the crime. One report, broadcast over police radio, describes a man fleeing the scene as a white male, twenty-seven, 5 feet, 11 inches, 165 pounds, black wavy hair, fair complected, white Eisenhower-type jacket, dark trousers, and white shirt—a description that does not match that of Oswald or his clothing. The man is said to be carrying a ".32 caliber dark finish *automatic*," a weapon much different than the revolver in Oswald's possession at the time of his arrest. Spent cartridge shells found at the scene are reported by a veteran officer to be from "an *automatic* .38 rather than a pistol." The vast difference between a .38 revolver and a .38 automatic cartridge is too great to be mis-identified by a veteran officer.

Also, it was later discovered that bullets removed from Officer Tippit's body did not match the Oswald revolver. Neither did these bullets match the spent cartridge shells that were turned in as evidence. Of the four bullets taken from Tippit's body, *one* was a Remington-Peters manufacture and *three* were made by Winchester-Western. On the contrary, of the spent cartridges, *two* were made by Winchester-Western and *two* by Remington-Peters.

Aquilla Clemons, another eyewitness, sees *two* men at the scene. These men, she reports, converse with hand signals and then depart in different directions.

Only two witnesses, Domingo Benavides and Helen Markham, claim to have seen the actual shooting. Benavides, who had perhaps the best view, could not identify Oswald as the killer and was not called to testify before the Warren Commission. Markham, however, was called and gave, at best, flimsy testimony. Six times, under questioning, Mrs. Markham denied recognizing any of the four men—which included Oswald—in the police lineup. Undeterred by her persistent denials, and after continued badgering, Commission

counsel finally gets the desired response as
Mrs. Markham states, ". . . I looked at him.
When I saw this man (Oswald) I wasn't sure,
but I had cold chills just run all over me."

Even though the evidence, as can be seen,
is conflicting and jerry-built, the Warren
Commission eventually uses it to establish
Oswald as the murderer of Officer Tippit.
They do so in order to bolster their case for
Oswald having shot the President. Oswald's
shooting of Tippit, they propose, demon-
strates his propensity to kill.

1:25 P.M.

Parkland Hospital—Dallas

Justice of the Peace Theron Ward arrives at
the emergency entrance of Parkland Hospital. He attempts to enter but is prevented
from doing so by several men in suits, whom
he assumes are Secret Service agents. Quickly
making his way around to the front entrance,
he is recognized by a woman at the front
desk who tells him the doctors are waiting
for him while she leads him back to the emergency room. Upon entering the area he is
immediately confronted by Dallas Coroner

Dr. Earl Rose. The frantic Dr. Rose, right arm upraised and finger pointing to the ceiling, shouts, "Ward, you are on the line!" Referring to the time in which a forensic examination could be made of President Kennedy, he continued, "We can have him out of here in forty-five minutes."

Instructions from pathology have already been given to operating room assistant supervisor Jane Wester for the preparation of a craniotomy (surgical cutting or removal of part of the skull for exploration) to be performed on the President. Dr. Rose is trained in forensic pathology (medical–legal examination preparatory to courtroom testimony) and was ready to carry out the laws of the state of Texas. It was his duty to examine the President's body, his clothes, and the scene of the crime. He was also charged with determining the number of shots, as well as establishing the direction from which they came.

Judge Ward is escorted to the door of Trauma Room 1 by Secret Service Agent Kellerman. Viewing the President's body from the doorway, he never enters the room. He notices a "plug" out of the front of Kennedy's head, as well as the tracheostomy opening in his throat. Kellerman requests Ward to release the body into Secret Service custody. The judge replies, "I will have to consult with Dallas District Attorney Henry Wade."

Calling Wade, Ward is told that, in Wade's opinion, a "missile" (bullet) must be taken into evidence and that Dallas Police Chief Curry should be queried on this point. Wade, in turn, calls Curry, confirming the opinion, and relays the information back to Ward. The judge mysteriously ignores the advice of the two Texas officials (to take possession of a bullet that may have killed the President) and releases the body to Kellerman. Without saying a word, Ward simply points to the exit, allowing Kellerman to begin removal of the body and all evidence associated therewith. Texas law was breached and a critical link in the investigative process violated.

1:26 P.M.

Love Field—Dallas

Police Chief Curry drives Lyndon Johnson to Love Field, where he boards *Air Force One* as the thirty-sixth President of the United States.

Parkland Hospital

When I walked back into the hall, Evalea Glanges, a medical student, was standing by the nurses' station. She told me a most peculiar story. While we had been working on President Kennedy, she was outside in the emergency room parking lot. Standing beside the President's limousine, she pointed out to another medical student that there was a bullet hole in the windshield. Upon over-hearing her comment, a Secret Service agent nervously jumped into the car and sped away.

The limousine had been at least partially cleaned while parked at Parkland Hospital. There is no record of any evidence found during this time.

The limousine was driven to Love Field and placed aboard a plane by Secret Service Agent Kinney. It arrives in Washington at 7:00 P.M. and is driven to the White House garage, where it is covered with a plastic sheet and guarded by agents.

At 9:10 P.M. the vehicle is inspected by representatives of the President's chief physician.

At 12:00 midnight, FBI agents, assisted by the Secret Service, examine the limousine. Several bullet fragments and a three-inch triangular piece of the President's skull are removed as evidence. A small hole just left of center in the windshield as well as a dent in the chrome molding strip above the windshield are noted. FBI agents state that the dent was made by a bullet fragment.

The bullet fragments taken from the limousine are not marked for identification. Six months later a Secret Service agent and a White House staffer were shown the crumpled fragments and were able to identify them as those found in the President's car shortly after the assassination. Of course, these fragments are linked to the Oswald rifle—a linkage that would never hold up in a court of law because of the broken chain in handling and marking this evidence.

Three days after the assassination, Carl Renas, head of security for the Dearborn Division of the Ford Motor Company, drives the limousine, helicopters hovering overhead, from Washington to Cincinnati. In doing so, he noted several bullet holes, the most notable being the one in the windshield's chrome molding strip, which he said was clearly "a primary strike" and "not a fragment."

The limousine was taken by Renas to Hess and Eisenhart in Cincinnati, where the chrome molding was replaced.

The Secret Service told Renas to "Keep your mouth shut."

Renas recalls thinking at the time, "Something is wrong."

The limousine was eventually rebuilt, bullet-proofed, and had incorporated into it every protective device known. However, President Johnson refused to use the car until its color was changed from its midnight blue—Kennedy blue—to standard black.

It is a shame and disgrace that evidentiary-gathering procedures were not followed with respect to the Presidential limousine. More shameful, however, is the fact that a vehicle of such historical significance—a virtual Ford's Theater—was not preserved. This was not a thoughtless act.

Glanges had also witnessed President Johnson and Lady Bird leaving for the airport. After they were rushed to an awaiting station wagon, the President crouched down in the backseat as the automobile left for Love Field. The front seat of the vehicle was loaded with worried Secret Service agents. Men in suits were everywhere. But they had good reason to be on edge. For all they knew, there was a plot to eliminate the entire hierarchy of the U.S. government, and the new President could be attacked at any moment. I must admit, the Cuban missile crisis of 1962 popped into my mind more than once that day.

The Secret Service's one and only job was to protect the President of the United States and other government officials around him, especially the Vice President. Having failed miserably at that task by allowing one Presidential assassination that

day, the agency's message was abundantly clear
to everyone—they wouldn't allow another one.

1:30 P.M.

Parkland Hospital—Dallas

Veteran newsman Seth Kantor, radio newsman Roy Stamps, and housewife Wilma Tice
see Jack Ruby at Parkland Hospital. Both
Kantor and Stamps have known Ruby for
many years. (In his testimony before the
Warren Commission, Ruby denies his presence there. The Commission chose to believe
Ruby despite evidence to the contrary. To do
otherwise might smack of conspiracy.)

1:33 P.M.

Love Field—Dallas

President Johnson boards *Air Force One* and
tells Colonel James B. Swindal that the aircraft will not leave for Washington without
President Kennedy's body.

Oak Cliff Section—Dallas

A Dallas police radio dispatch reports, "He is in the library, Jefferson, East 500 block, Marsalis and Jefferson." Minutes later, a follow-up dispatch says, "We are all at the library." Again, minutes later, *"It was the wrong man."*

Who is this suspect, so quickly apprehended and just as quickly dismissed as "the wrong man"? At this early stage, the only way they could have known it is the *wrong* man would be for them to know the *right* man.

The library, located at the intersection of East Jefferson Street and Marsalis Avenue, is six blocks from Oswald's rooming house and within only one block of Ruby's apartment. Oswald is known to have frequented this library at least three to four times a week.

Just as it has never been clear as to exactly how Oswald was so quickly known to be in the Texas Theatre, it is still unclear why the police were so quickly dispatched to this library. Was some unknown hand guiding authorities toward Oswald?

Parkland Hospital—Dallas

A distraught Malcolm Kilduff, White House Press Secretary, holds a press conference at Parkland Hospital. He announces the time of the President's death as 1:00 and says that "He died of a gunshot wound in the brain." When asked by a newsman to elaborate on the cause of death, Kilduff points to his right temple and replies, "Dr. Burkley told me it, it's a simple matter . . . of a bullet right through the head."

Parkland Hospital—Dallas

As Glanges and I continued to talk, a bronze casket was being wheeled toward Trauma Room 1 by two male employees from the Oneal Funeral Home. I opened the door, allowing them to enter, then followed them in. I was the only doctor in the room. All of the tubes had been removed from the President, his body had been cleaned, and he had been wrapped in two white sheets. The casket was opened, and two nurses placed a plastic-mattress covering over the white-velvet lining to keep any blood that might still seep from the wounds from staining the material.

Before I directed that the body be moved, I turned down the sheet and took one long, last look at President Kennedy's head wound. I was the last doctor at Parkland Hospital to see it. After making my final examination, I lightly stroked his reddish-brown hair. I felt so terribly sorry for him. He was handsome, intelligent, charismatic, young—and the tragedy that had befallen him overwhelmed me.

Four of us lifted the President into the casket and placed his neatly folded clothes at his feet. As the two men sealed the coffin, it seemed strange to feel such a closeness to a man whom I had never known, other than through the news media. As I watched the handles being slowly turned to tighten the lid, I wondered who had done this to the President, and what effect it would have on our country.

It wasn't until years later, when I saw the autopsy pictures of John Kennedy taken at the Bethesda Naval Hospital, that I realized there was something rotten in America in 1963. The very last, and most alarming, thought one wants to have of his government is that he cannot trust the people who run it. But that is exactly what I believed when I examined the official autopsy photographs taken in Maryland on November 22, 1963.

The doctors there had recorded the condition of John F. Kennedy's cranium, a state that had substantially changed during a period of six hours and over a distance of 1,500 miles. Great effort had been made to reconstruct the back of the President's head, and the incision Perry had made in his throat at Parkland for the tracheostomy had been enlarged and mangled, as if someone had conducted another procedure. It looked to be the work of a butcher. No doubt, someone had gone to a great deal of trouble to show a different story than we had seen at Parkland.

More disturbingly, there were two eyewitnesses present at the autopsy, James Jenkins and Paul O'Connor, who swear that President Kennedy arrived at the Naval medical facility zipped in a gray body bag inside a different coffin—one of cheap material. And even more astounding, these men, who have gone through numerous tests and substantial harassment to be proclaimed credible, claim there was no brain when the body came out of the gray bag. As the last doctor to see President Kennedy before his body left Parkland, I can unequivocally report that there was no gray body bag, and that he still had the left side of his brain.

The "Warren Commission Report" is also mysterious to me. As I watched the President's loosening grip on life, I had absolutely no doubt that I was viewing two frontal-entry bullet wounds. Had we turned him over, we would have discovered a third entry wound in his back, between the shoulder blades. And beyond absurdity is the magic bullet theory, postulating that a missile traveled through President Kennedy's neck, then traversed Governor Connally's torso, whereupon it shattered his wrist, and finally lodged deeply within his thigh.

Macabre and tabloid-style stories have purported that John Kennedy is alive in the basement of Parkland Hospital. As a physician, I know life from death, and when I helped place President Kennedy in that casket, he was *dead*.

1:40 P.M

Oak Cliff Section—Dallas

Lee Harvey Oswald enters the Texas Theatre on East Jefferson Street in the Oak Cliff section of town.

1:45 P.M.
Parkland Hospital—Dallas: The "Magic" Bullet"

Hospital engineer Darrell Tomlinson discovers an intact bullet on a stretcher and turns it over to hospital security director O.P. Wright. Wright attempts to turn over custody of the bullet to an FBI agent, who refuses to accept it. He then gives it to Secret Service Agent Richard Johnson. (Both Tomlinson and Wright, when later shown the bullet alleged to be the one discovered at Parkland Hospital, declined to identify it as the one they handled that day. Only Tomlinson was ever questioned by the Warren Commission about this strategic piece of evidence found a short time *after* Jack Ruby's appearance at the hospital.)

This bullet, defying all logic and flying in the face of all rules of evidence, was to become the major link between the assassination and suspect Oswald. The Warren Commission, in its haste to label Oswald as the sole rifleman firing from a position behind the President, created the following impossible scenario:

Oswald fires from the sixth-floor southeasternmost window of the Book Depository.

The missile strikes the President in the upper back near his spine, exiting his throat just below the Adam's apple. Then, while pausing in midair, it turns right, then left, then downward, entering the governor's back below the right shoulder blade near his armpit. The bullet continues on its fabricated path through Connally's chest, shattering his fifth rib and exiting just below his right nipple. The missile then enters the outer forearm near the wrist, splintering the large radius bone, exiting the inner forearm, and finally embedding itself in Governor Connally's left thigh. From here, this miracle-working missile disengages itself, cleans itself of any trace of blood or tissue, and in unmutilated, almost perfect condition, buries itself under the mat of an emergency room stretcher.

This implausible theory was presented to the American people as fact and portrayed Lee Harvey Oswald as the lone, unaided killer of the President. In doing so, the Warren Commission had to ignore the missile's broken chain of evidence, utilize an illusionary bullet trajectory, and approve obvious wound fabrication or alteration of the President's body.

1:50 P.M.

Texas Theatre—Oak Cliff Section of Dallas

Lee Harvey Oswald is arrested at the Texas Theatre and taken to the Dallas police headquarters. The circumstances of his apprehension are intriguing.

Johnny Brewer, manager of a shoe store near the theater, observes Oswald go into the movie house without paying, and notifies the theater cashier. The cashier, Julia Postal, did not see Oswald enter the theater but relates the incident to concession operator W. H. Burroughs. Burroughs states that he heard the front doors open but saw no one come past him through the lobby. Assuming that Oswald had taken the stairs to the balcony, Postal calls the police.

Within minutes, several cars of police (about fifteen officers), FBI Agents Robert Barrett and Bardwell Odum, together with Dallas Assistant District Attorney Bill Alexander, converge on the theater—all to capture a man suspected of entering the theater without paying. The house lights are turned up and the authorities enter the theater. Ten to fifteen people are scattered throughout the room. One of them, a man sitting near the front, tells Officer M. N. McDonald, "The man you want is sitting in the third row from the rear, not in the balcony." McDonald moves cautiously down the aisle, crouching low, gun drawn, toward Oswald. However, he stops about midway to talk to two people. Oswald stands up as McDonald approaches and a scuffle ensues. Other officers join in subduing Oswald and drag him, protesting, from the theater and place him in an awaiting police car.

Johnny Brewer witnesses the arrest and sees "Fists flying . . . they were hitting him," and hears some of the police holler, "Kill the President, will you." Julia Postal allows a police officer to use her box-office phone and hears him remark, "I think we have got our man on both accounts." S. L. Reed, taking pictures of the incident outside the theater, overhears an officer state that Oswald "killed the President."

George Applin not only witnesses the arrest of Oswald, but also sees Jack Ruby inside the theater.

Many questions arise regarding the quick apprehension of Lee Harvey Oswald. Why did so many officers respond to a one-man gate crasher? Why did an assistant district attorney leave the Book Depository murder site to accompany officers to the theater? Why did an FBI agent participate in the ar-

rest, which at that time could only be surmised as a local misdemeanor? Why were the
arresting officers already proclaiming the capture of the murderer of both President Kennedy and Officer Tippit? More important,
was Jack Ruby at the scene? And if so, why?
Could it have been Ruby himself who points
out Oswald to arresting officers?

1:57 P.M.

Dealey Plaza—Dallas

Lee Bowers, still at his position in the railroad tower near Dealey Plaza, reports to Dallas officers that a man is hiding in a railroad
car. Bowers had stopped the train after ob-
serving the suspicious-acting man "hunkered
down" inside the open-top car. Several officers proceed to the area and, with arms
drawn, apprehend three men. The three men
are taken to the nearby Sheriff's office and
are later turned over to Captain Will Fritz of
the Dallas Police Department. The men were
never booked, and no official record exists
of their having ever been questioned. (Later,
when Fritz is questioned about the disposition of the three suspicious characters, he re-

plies, "If you talk to the FBI they might help you . . . that's the only ones who'd have it.")

Parkland Hospital—Dallas

As though on cue, a phalanx of guards poured into Trauma Room 1 just as the coffin was being rolled out. They looked like a swarm of locusts descending upon a cornfield. Without any discussion, they encircled the casket and began escorting the President's body down the hall toward the emergency room exit. A man in a suit, leading the group, holding a submachine gun, left little doubt in my mind who was in charge. That he wasn't smiling best describes the look on his face. Just outside Trauma Room 1, Jacqueline joined the escort and placed her hand on the coffin as she walked along beside it. I followed directly behind them.

When the entourage had moved into the main hall, Dr. Earl Rose, chief of forensic pathology, confronted the men in suits. Roy Kellerman, the man leading the group, looked sternly at Dr. Rose and announced, "My friend, this is the body of the President of the United States, and we are going to take it back to Washington."

Dr. Rose bristled and replied, "No, that's not the way things are. When there's a homicide, we must have an autopsy."

"He's the President. He's going with us," Kellerman barked, with increased intensity in his voice.

"The body stays," Dr. Rose said with equal poignancy.

Kellerman took an erect stance and brought his firearm into a ready position. The other men in suits followed course by draping their coattails behind the butts of their holstered pistols. How brave of these men, wearing their Brooks Brothers suits with icons of distinction (color-coded Secret Service buttons) pinned to their lapels, willing to shoot an unarmed doctor to secure a corpse.

"My friend, my name is Roy Kellerman. I am special agent in charge of the White House detail of the Secret Service. We are taking President Kennedy back to the capitol."

"You are not taking the body anywhere. There's a law here. We're going to enforce it."

Admiral George Burkley, White House Medical Officer, said, 'Mrs. Kennedy is going to stay exactly where she is until the body is moved. We can't have that ... he's the President of the United States."

"That doesn't matter," Dr. Rose replied rigidly. "You can't lose the chain of evidence."

For the second time that day, there was little doubt in my mind as to the significance of what was happening before me.

"Goddammit, get your ass out of the way before you get hurt," screamed another one of the men in suits. Another snapped, "We're taking the body, now."

Strange, I thought, this President is getting more protection dead than he did when he was alive.

Had Dr. Rose not stepped aside, I'm sure that those thugs would have shot him. They would have killed me and anyone else who got in their way. Dr. Kemp Clark wanted to physically detain the coffin, but the men with guns acted like tough guys with specific orders. A period of twenty-seven years has neither erased the fear that I felt nor diminished the impression that that incident made upon me.

They loaded the casket into the hearse, Jacqueline got into the backseat, placed her hand on top of the coffin, and bowed her head. As they drove off, I felt that a thirty-year-old surgeon had seen more than his share for one day. My wristwatch read 2:08 P.M.

2:15 P.M.

Love Field—Dallas

President Kennedy's body is placed aboard *Air Force One*. Jacqueline Kennedy accompanies the casket, remaining with it at all times except for the short period she is in attendance while Johnson is given the Presidential oath.

City Hall—Dallas

Officers arrive at the jail, located on the upper floors of City Hall, with suspect Lee

Harvey Oswald. Oswald's forehead shows a fresh abrasion and his left eye is bruised and swollen. His clothes and hair are disheveled. It is apparent that his arrest had come only after a fight. He is taken to the interrogation room by Detectives Richard Sims and Elmer Boyd.

Upon the announcement that the President's killer had been apprehended, and that his name was Lee Harvey Oswald, FBI Agent James Hosty quickly heads to Dallas Police Headquarters. Oswald was well known to the agent and had been assigned to him upon Oswald's move to the Dallas area. In the weeks prior to the President's visit, Agent Hosty had made two unsuccessful attempts to contact Oswald. He had only been able to speak with Oswald's wife, Marina, and her close friend, Ruth Paine. Oswald, on the other hand, had attempted to make contact with Hosty and had delivered a note to the agent's secretary at FBI headquarters.

As Agent Hosty races up the stairs toward the interrogation room where Oswald is being held, he is joined by Police Lieutenant Jack Revill. Hosty tells Revill, "We knew that Lee Harvey Oswald was capable of assassinating the President of the United States, but we didn't dream he would do it." The meaning of this cryptic comment has never been adequately explained. On the surface, however, it appears to be another hasty attempt to place the blame for the murder on the "lone nut," Lee Harvey Oswald. Agent Hosty was eventually forced to deny making the statement to Revill or face the question, why, if Oswald was a known threat to the President, did the FBI never alert the Secret Service? Hosty must have known from his previous contacts with Oswald's wife and her friend Ruth Paine that Oswald was employed at the Texas School Book Depository, overlooking the motorcade route. Mrs. Paine had been instrumental in helping Oswald acquire this job.

2:20 P.M.

Captain Fritz has Oswald brought from the interrogation room to his office in the Homicide and Robbery division. Present in the office with Fritz are Detectives Sims and Boyd, FBI Agents James Bookhout, James Hosty, and Joe Meyers, and a Secret Service agent. Oswald is asked if he worked for the Texas School Book Depository. He replied that he did. When asked what part of the building he was in at the time the President was shot, he stated that he was having lunch on the second floor.

2:30 P.M.

Captain Fritz orders three of his detectives to meet sheriff's deputies at the home of Ruth Paine in the nearby city of Irving. This is the location where Oswald's wife had been staying. The officers are to search the premises.

Parkland Hospital—Dallas

I went up to Operating Room 5 on the second floor to watch Drs. Robert R. Shaw, professor of thoracic surgery, and James Boland and James "Red" Duke, residents in thoracic surgery, operate on Governor Connally's chest. Diagnosis of his thoracic condition was a single gunshot wound to the chest with comminuted fracture of the fifth rib, laceration of the middle lobe, and hematoma of the lower lobe of the right lung. After one hour and forty-five minutes of surgery, Drs. Charles F. Gregory, professor of orthopedic surgery, and William Osborn, orthopedic resident, operated on the arm. Simultaneously Drs. Shires, Baxter, McClellan, and Don Patman, senior resident in surgery, worked on the left thigh. I observed Dr. Osborn remove at least five bullet fragments from the governor's arm and handed them to Nurse Audrey Bell. A bullet fragment in the governor's left thigh was not removed, because it was not a threat at this location. Total operating time was three hours and fifty minutes. All surgery on Governor Connally ceased at 4:45 P.M. From surgery, he was taken to the recovery room, where an intensive-care area was established by partitioning the room with sheets. This was well before the sophistication of modern intensive-care units and equipment.

2:38 P.M.

Love Field—Dallas

Aboard *Air Force One* preparations have been made to give the oath of office to Lyndon Johnson. Dallas Federal Judge Sarah T. Hughes, a Johnson appointee, has been called in to administer the oath. President Kennedy's personal Bible is removed from his private cabin and used in the ceremony. Mrs. Kennedy stands beside Johnson, still in her pink blood-soaked suit. Judge Hughes is shaking but manages to get through the twenty-eight-second oath.

3:30 P.M.

Paine Home—Irving

Officers arrive at the residence of Michael and Ruth Paine at 2515 West Fifth Street in Irving. Mrs. Paine greets the officers at the door and indicates she has been expecting them. Inviting them in, she agrees to a search of the house. Officers do so and in the garage they find a blanket said to have been used to wrap a rifle, but the rifle is gone. Mr. Paine arrives home from work during this time.

There are many unanswered questions about the role of Michael and Ruth Paine in the lives of Lee and Marina Oswald. However, none raises more interest than an FBI report of a telephone conversation between the couple on the day following the President's death. Mr. Paine is heard to comment that he felt sure Oswald had killed the President but did not feel that he was responsible. Paine further stated, *"We both know who is responsible."* This statement indicates that the Paines possessed knowledge that someone with whom they were familiar was manipulating or directing Oswald. Though this information was in the hands of the FBI, neither of the Paines was ever officially asked to name this mysterious "responsible" person.

4:00 P.M.

Aboard Air Force One

Somewhere high over the United States, the new President receives news that the assassination is the act of one lone individual and that NO CONSPIRACY EXISTS. The information comes, not from Dallas, but from the nation's capitol. Specifically, it came from either McGeorge Bundy or Commander Oliver Hallet in the Situation Room of the White House Communications Center.

4:35 P.M.

City Hall—Dallas

Oswald is taken by officers to the show-up room for the first of several lineups. Oddly, though he had been searched at the time of his arrest, Detectives Boyd and Sims decide to search him again. In Oswald's pockets they find five live rounds of .38 ammunition and a bus transfer slip.

Tippit-shooting-witness Helen Markham views the lineup of Oswald and three others and gives her very shaky identification.

5:10 P.M.

Andrews Air Force Base—Bethesda, Maryland

At Andrews Air Force Base, the coffin is placed into an ambulance for its trip to Bethesda Naval Hospital, where the autopsy will be performed. Robert Kennedy, Jacqueline, and General Godfrey McHugh sit in the rear of the automobile with the casket. President Johnson and his entourage leave aboard helicopters for the White House.

Parkland Hospital—Dallas

Although I was technically off duty, I stayed with Connally to help change the governor's dressings and monitor certain laboratory values. I had been closely following research into the coagulation problem of trauma victims. Because of my interest in this area of medicine, Dr. Shires allowed me to assist him on the governor's case.

Prothrombin, a substance produced by the liver, is one of the factors that promotes clotting. When blood loss is extensive, this clotting agent can be depleted, requiring that the patient be given vitamin K, which is used by the liver to produce prothrombin. The governor's prothrombin time was prolonged and low, which exposed him to additional bleeding.

6:00 P.M.
City Hall—Dallas

WFAA radio and television reporter Victor Robertson, Jr., stands in the hall near the entrance to Captain Fritz's third-floor office. Two police officers are guarding the door. Robertson sees Jack Ruby approach and attempt to enter the office. He is prevented from doing so by one of the officers who says, "You can't go in there, Jack." Ruby makes a joking remark and heads back down the hall toward the elevator.

6:30 P.M.
City Hall—Dallas

Again Oswald is taken to the show-up room. Bus driver Cecil McWatters identifies Oswald as a passenger on his bus shortly after the assassination. Ted Calloway and

Sam Guinyard state that Oswald is the person they saw running, gun in hand, from the scene of the shooting of Officer Tippit.

7:00 P.M.

Marina Oswald and Mr. and Mrs. Paine are brought into police headquarters. Shown the rifle allegedly found on the sixth floor of the Book Depository, Marina states that it is "like" her husband's but that she is "not sure." Officers take her affidavit.

7:00 P.M.

Bethesda Naval Hospital—Bethesda, Maryland

President Kennedy's body has been transferred from the casket to the eight-foot-long autopsy table in the center of the morgue's main chamber. Present in the room are no less than twenty-eight people. Among those crowded into the area are the President's personal physician, agents from the FBI and Secret Service, the commanding officer of the

Naval Medical Center, and the surgeon general of the Navy.

Commander J. J. Humes, the Director of Laboratories of the National Medical School at the Naval Medical Center in Bethesda, chooses J. T. Boswell, M.D., chief of pathology and P. A. Finck, M.D., chief of wound ballistics pathology, Armed Forces Institute of Pathology at Walter Reed Medical Center, Washington, to assist him in performing the autopsy. None of the three men was a practicing forensic pathologist or had special expertise in examining bullet wounds.

In 1979, the House Select Committee on Assassinations investigated the records of the President's postmortem examination and reported it to be fraught with procedural errors. They charged the following:

1. The President's body was taken out of the hands of those responsible for investigation of the death and autopsy—Texas authorities.
2. Those performing the autopsy had insufficient training and experience to evaluate a death from gunshot wounds.
3. Physicians who treated the President at Parkland Hospital were not consulted before commencing the autopsy.
4. Circumstances at the time of autopsy were not controlled by the pathologist.

5. Proper photographs were not taken.
6. The President's clothing was not examined.
7. The autopsy procedure was incomplete because:
   a. External examination failed to accurately locate wounds.
   b. The bullet tracks were not dissected to determine their course through the body.
   c. The angles of the bullet tracks through the body were not measured relative to the body axis.
   d. The brain was not properly examined and sectioned.
8. The report was incomplete, inaccurate, and prepared without reference to photographs.
9. The head wound location was incorrect.
10. Other wounds of the President's body were not localized with reference to fixed body landmarks so as to permit reconstruction of trajectories.

These glaring procedural inaccuracies and errors are blamed on the inexperience of the autopsy team. But was inexperience and improper procedure the culprit—or was the autopsy purposefully falsified in order to frame Oswald as the lone assassin and declare NO CONSPIRACY? Much can be learned concerning this question by carefully analyzing the testimony of doctors and aides at Parkland Hospital. A comparison of what they observed of the President's wounds with those reported by the Bethesda autopsy team reveals irreconcilable discrepancies. Consider the following:

1. At Parkland Hospital the wound to the right side of the President's head is a large, gaping hole extending from the temple area all the way around to the back of the head. At Bethesda Naval Hospital, the back of the President's head is intact, with only a small puncture just to the right of midline near the base of the skull. The large gaping hole is *only* on the upper right side, with no damage to the rear of the head.

2. At Parkland Hospital, a small wound of entry is seen in the President's throat just below his Adam's apple and slightly enlarged to accommodate the tracheal tube. Upon examination at Bethesda, this wound has become a three-inch-wide gaping gash.

3. At Bethesda, pathologists discover a wound in the President's upper back near the spine. Parkland Hospital doctors were not aware of this wound. In their frantic but futile attempt to resusci-

tate the President, they never turned him over to examine his back.

Another of the more important evidentiary aspects of any investigation involving gunshots are the bullets and bullet fragments connected with the crime. In this area, as with the postmortem examination of the President, the evidence is incomplete, distorted, and outright erroneous.

Cases in point are:

1. The Stretcher Bullet:
This so-called magic bullet is discussed elsewhere in this book. As has already been shown, this bullet could not later be identified by its finders, Tomlinson and Wright. Neither could it later be identified by Richard Johnson, the Secret Service agent who received it, nor the man Johnson released it to, Secret Service Chief James Rowley.

There were *no* residues of blood or tissue on the bullet and it was obviously a "plant." At this late date, it is difficult to understand how such a fabrication could ever have been put forth as theory, let alone fact. But, the reality is, powerful and learned men *did* place this flawed theory into the public record as fact. Upon recognizing this, one is then forced to question the motive and intent of those responsible for such a fable.

2. Bullet Fragments:

The Warren Commission received *two* bullet fragments that were "found in the front of the President's car." One fragment was from a portion of a bullet's nose area, whereas the second was from "a bullet's base portion." These fragments were badly mutilated, and it could not be determined whether they were portions of a single bullet or were two separate bullets. Both of these fragments *did* possess residues of blood.

Three small lead fragments are found in the floorboard of the rear of the limousine. One of these fragments is reported missing in 1970.

Though these fragments are said to be from the Oswald rifle, their finding, handling, and identification are questionable.

At the President's autopsy, three small fragments are removed from the President's head. X-rays show many minute fragments scattered throughout the skull.

3. Whole Missiles:

Two FBI agents present during the President's autopsy, James Sibert and Francis O'Neil, receive and sign a receipt for a "missile removed during the examination of the body." The receipt is in the official record though the missile itself has never been entered into evidence.

Captain David Osborne, Chief of Surgery at Bethesda, was also present at the autopsy. He recalls seeing an "intact slug" (a missile) fall out on to the autopsy table as the President's clothing was moved.

Back at Dallas, in Dealey Plaza just after the assassination, an FBI agent picks up a bullet in the grass just beyond the south curb of Elm Street a few feet from where the President was slain. Photographs at the time clearly reveal the agent bending to pick up the bullet and then placing it in his trousers pocket. The bullet is never seen again and no report is found in the official record. However, alert newsmen, as well as photographers, have documented its existence. The November 23 edition of the *Dallas Times-Herald* reports: "Dallas Police Lt. J. C. Day of the Crime Lab estimated the distance from the sixth floor window the slayer used to the spot where *one of the bullets* was recovered, at 100 yards." The magazine *New Republic* of December 21 stated: ". . . police officers were examining the area at the side of the street where the President was hit, and a police inspector told me *they had just found another bullet in the grass."*

4. Governor Connally:

As determined by x-rays, Governor Connally continues to have two small fragments in his body. They were never removed during his treatment at Parkland Hospital. Officially, only three very small fragments were removed from the governor. This is disputed, however, by operating room nurse Audrey Bell. She states that four to six small- to medium-size fragments were handed to her by doctors treating Connally's wounds. Her statement is confirmed by Texas Department of Public Safety Officer Charles Harbison, who received the fragments from Bell, then passed them on to the FBI. The House Select Committee on Assassinations' report concerning these fragments stated that "The method of labeling and handling this evidence was so poor that there might have been difficulty in having it admitted as evidence in a criminal procedure."

To further complicate matters, the governor's clothes, of primary importance to the investigation, were laundered by person or persons unknown, prior to being turned over to authorities.

The House Select Committee on Assassinations, while reinvestigating the circumstances surrounding the assassination of President Kennedy, chose to verify the original Warren Commission findings concerning the medical and ballistics evidence. It did so despite missing and poor-quality autopsy photographs, unverified x-rays, missing tissue slides of the wound areas, lack of probe or dissection of the wounds, no sectioning of the brain, and the burning of original autopsy notes. (These original autopsy notes were burned by Commander Humes, the chief pathologist, in the fireplace of his home on Sunday morning following the assassination. There has never been a reasonable explanation for this act.) The Committee's conclusion, therefore, is based on tainted evidence, manipulated trajectories, and a false autopsy. It ignored, or labeled erroneous, all testimony and evidence that they found in conflict with the lone-assassin scenario created by their predecessor, the Warren Commission.

Concerning the missing autopsy materials, the Committee reports ". . . evidence tends to show that Robert Kennedy either destroyed these materials or *otherwise rendered them inaccessible*." Could Robert Kennedy, the President's brother, have been making preparations to investigate his brother's death should he himself become President? Before an audience of students at San Fernando State College in California on June 3, 1968, three days before his own assassination, he stated, "Only the powers of the Presidency will reveal the secrets of my brother's death."

After Robert's death, Evelyn Lincoln, President Kennedy's personal secretary, became concerned about the disposition of the autopsy materials. To make certain that the family was aware of their existence, Ted Kennedy was contacted. He replied that everything was under control.

7:03 P.M.

City Hall—Dallas

Oswald is arraigned before Justice of the Peace David Johnston for the murder of Officer Tippit. Captain Fritz signs the complaint. Assistant District Attorney Bill Alexander is present.

7:55 P.M.

Jeannette and Virginia Davis, residents near the Tippit murder scene, are brought into the show-up room. Oswald makes his third appearance in a lineup. The Davises identify Oswald as the man they saw unloading a pistol as he cut across their yard immediately following the shooting.

8:55 P.M.

Detectives J. B. Hicks and Robert Studebaker take Oswald to the Homicide and Robbery Office for fingerprinting. A few minutes later, Detective Pete Barnes comes in, and the three crime lab men make paraffin casts of Oswald's hands and right cheek. (The tests came back positive for his hands and negative for his right cheek, indicating that Oswald *may* have fired a pistol but *not* a rifle.)

9:00 P.M.

Buell Wesley Frazier and his sister, Minnie Randle, are brought in to Homicide and Robbery and give affidavits. Oswald had ridden to the Book Depository with Frazier on the morning of the assassination. Both state that Oswald was carrying a package with him at the time.

9:30 P.M.

Downtown Dallas

An attendant at Nichol's Parking Garage next door to Ruby's Carousel Club receives a phone call from Jack Ruby. Ruby requests the attendant to give one of his strippers, Little Lynn, five dollars in cash, stating he will reimburse him when he comes to the club a short time later. The attendant complies with the request, but asks the stripper to sign a small piece of scratch-pad paper as a receipt for the money. This is the first time Ruby has ever made such a request of the attendant.

Approximately thirty minutes to an hour later, Ruby arrives at the garage and reimburses the attendant. In doing so, he also makes an unusual request that the garage attendant stamp Little Lynn's signed receipt in the garage's automatic time clock. Again the attendant complies with Ruby's request, and the receipt is dated and timed, "1963 Nov 23 PM 10:33." Ruby leaves the garage and heads for City Hall a few blocks away.

11:00 P.M.

Oswald is placed in a jail cell.

Bethesda Naval Hospital—Bethesda, Maryland

At Bethesda, the autopsy of President Kennedy continues. Nearby, Robert Kennedy and family friends await the results.

Parkland Hospital—Dallas

While we waited for test results, Dr. Duke and I drank coffee, smoked cigarettes, and compared notes on our most amazing day. I remember stopping in the anesthesia call room several times that night to watch the nonstop news coverage of the Presidential assassination. We had seen the undoing of many careers that day, especially those of Secret Service agents. And it was apparent to me that other people, mostly reporters, were capitalizing on the tragedy to further their professions. I do not believe that we at Parkland, and I in particular, fit into that category, as evidenced by my waiting twenty-seven years before writing this book. Most of the doctors who were there are nearing retirement age. If we had intended to use that experience to further our media opportunities, we would have begun long before now.

When the lab results indicated that Governor Connally's prothrombin time had been reestablished and was within the normal limits, I decided to go home. As I emerged from the hospital and walked into the parking lot, my legs felt weak, and a blustery north wind chilled me down to the bone. But the icy sensation that troubled me the most had nothing to do with weather. Rather, it had to do with the abrupt change of our government in the time it took to squeeze a trigger.

Orderly succession or not, the United States of America would never again be the same. A new course for the country had already been set in the mind of the new President, who, although a Democrat, had different ideas, opinions, and dreams than his predecessor. I sensed that a day would not go by that I wouldn't, in some way, relive the experience. Yet, must I determine if I was fortunate for the insight and sensitivity that comes from such an ordeal, or cursed with a scarred memory of the horror and fear of it all.

As soon as I arrived at the apartments, neighbors and friends descended upon me to learn what had happened at Parkland. I was very careful about what I told them, because I sensed there would be several accounts of the assassination. More than anything else, I wanted to learn the facts about who had done it and the way it was accomplished before I said too much, even to curious outsiders. The look on the face of the man with the machine gun still bothered me. I didn't want to cross paths with him ever again.

After several hours of giving an edited account of my day, everyone left and my wife went to bed. It was 2:00 A.M. I remember reading a medical journal for about an hour to take my mind off the assassination. It is difficult to unwind after witnessing the death of the President of the United States. As I

Dr. Charles Crenshaw. *(CREDIT: Susan L. Crenshaw)*

Dr. Crenshaw in 1988.
(Photo courtesy of Susan L. Crenshaw)

Dr. Crenshaw, right, in the surgical suite.
(Photo courtesy of Susan L. Crenshaw)

Aerial view—Dealey Plaza, Dallas, Texas. *(CREDIT: J. Gary Shaw)*

Official autopsy photographs of President Kennedy taken at Bethesda Naval Hospital. *(CREDIT: Paul O'Connor)*

There was a small entry wound to the President's throat when he arrived at the hospital. A small incision was made at this wound for insertion of a tracheotomy. The wound appears to have been greatly enlarged and does not reflect its condition upon leaving Parkland Hospital.

Top view of the President's head.

Left profile of the President's head.

Rear view of the President's head showing no damage to the area. This is incorrect. This area contained a large exit wound.

The President's back appears to show two wounds. These were not observed at Parkland because the back was not examined. This wound(s) was not dissected during autopsy in order to determine its course through the body. Therefore, angles of the bullet(s)' track through the body were not measured relative to the body axis.

Rear seat of the Presidential limousine shortly after the assassination. The President's blood and brains cover the seat.
(CREDIT: National Archives)

Texas School Book Depository within seconds of the shooting. James Powell of Army Intelligence took the photograph. First window from the right, second floor from the top, is the alleged window from which the shots were fired. Same floor, first window from the left, is where Arnold Rowland saw a man with a rifle shortly before the President arrived in the area. (CREDIT: FBI, J. Gary Shaw Collection)

The infamous "Magic Bullet." This missile is credited with causing seven wounds to two men while having sustained little damage itself. A physical impossibility.

CERTIFICATION OF VITAL RECORD

TEXAS DEPARTMENT OF HEALTH
BUREAU OF VITAL STATISTICS

CERTIFICATE OF DEATH

75708

PLACE OF DEATH		USUAL RESIDENCE	
Dallas		District of Columbia	COUNTY
Dallas	LENGTH OF STAY 2 Hrs.	Washington	
Parkland Memorial		1600 Pennsylvania Avenue	
		IS RESIDENCE INSIDE CITY LIMITS? YES☒ NO☐	IS RESIDENCE ON A FARM? YES☐ NO☒

NAME OF DECEASED	John	Fitzgerald	Kennedy	DATE OF DEATH November 22, 1963
SEX Male	COLOR OR RACE White	Married☒ Never Married☐ Widowed☐ Divorced☐	DATE OF BIRTH May 29, 1917	AGE 46
USUAL OCCUPATION President of the U.S.	KIND OF BUSINESS OR INDUSTRY United States Govt.		BIRTHPLACE Brookline, Mass.	CITIZEN OF WHAT COUNTRY U.S.A.
FATHER'S NAME Joseph P. Kennedy			MOTHER'S MAIDEN NAME Rose Fitzgerald	
WAS DECEASED EVER IN U.S. ARMED FORCES? YES WW II		SOCIAL SECURITY NO.	INFORMANT Evelyn Lincoln	

TEXAS DEPARTMENT OF HEALTH
REC'D. JAN 18 1964
BUREAU OF VITAL STATISTICS

CAUSE OF DEATH
IMMEDIATE CAUSE Multiple gunshot wounds of the head & neck.   Minutes

DUE TO

PART II. OTHER SIGNIFICANT CONDITIONS CONTRIBUTING TO DEATH BUT NOT RELATED TO THE TERMINAL DISEASE CONDITION GIVEN IN PART (a)   WAS AUTOPSY PERFORMED? YES☒ NO☐

ACCIDENT ☐	SUICIDE ☐	HOMICIDE ☒	DESCRIBE HOW INJURY OCCURRED Shot by a high powered rifle
TIME OF INJURY 12:31	Month 11	Day 22	Year 63
PLACE OF INJURY 400 Blk Elm St. Dallas, Tex	CITY, TOWN OR LOCATION Dallas	COUNTY Dallas	STATE Texas

I hereby certify that I Held Inquest
DATE November 22, 1963   Death occurred at 1:00 P.
SIGNATURE Theron Ward J.P.   305 N. 5th St. - Garland, Texas   DATE SIGNED 12-6-63

BURIAL, CREMATION, REMOVAL Removal	DATE 11-22-63	NAME OF CEMETERY OR CREMATORY Arlington National Cemetery
LOCATION Washington, D.C.		FUNERAL DIRECTOR'S SIGNATURE
		O'Neal Inc. VB O'Neal

| REGISTRAR'S FILE NO 6820 | DATE REC'D BY LOCAL REGISTRAR Dec 11, 1963 | REGISTRAR'S SIGNATURE J W Bass BY Maurine Lamon Acting Registrar |

This is to certify that this is a true and correct reproduction of the original record as recorded in this office. Issued under authority of Sec. 191.051, Health and Safety Code.

ISSUED   JUL 18 1990

Richard B. Bays
RICHARD B. BAYS
STATE REGISTRAR

WARNING: IT IS ILLEGAL TO DUPLICATE THIS COPY.

ANY ALTERATION OR ERASURE VOIDS THIS CERTIFICATE

Death certificate of President John F. Kennedy. Note the certification, "Held Inquest, November 22, 1963," signed by Dallas Justice of the Peace Theron Ward. No official inquest was ever held. Also, autopsy is checked "yes" when no autopsy was actually performed.

The alleged assassin, Lee Harvey Oswald. This photo showing Oswald dressed in all black, armed with two weapons, and holding Russian newspapers was used by authorities and media to help convince the public of Oswald's guilt. The photo bears indications of fakery. *(CREDIT: National Archives)*

Lee Harvey Oswald in death at the morgue.
(CREDIT: National Archives)

read, I asked myself over and over again, "How will you ever top this? Where do you go from here?" The answer that came roaring back each time was, "Back to work in three hours."

Before heading for bed, I turned on the television for a few minutes to find out what was happening. All three networks were still on the air. For the first time, I saw Lee Harvey Oswald and heard how he had allegedly shot the President from the sixth floor of the Texas School Book Depository Building. When they showed the President riding in his limousine, waving to the crowd, it was hard for me to believe that I had, only hours before, watched him die and then embraced his mourning wife.

As I shuffled to the bathroom in the dark, just as I had done twenty-three hours earlier, I was physically and emotionally exhausted. Too soon, I would rise to begin another surgical shift that wouldn't end until Sunday at 9:00 A.M. I stopped and kissed my son on his forehead. Life was zooming by, and I was missing being part of my son's life, but what could I do?

I closed the door, turned on the light, and looked into the mirror. The face staring at me looked ten years older than it had appeared the previous morning. Shaking my head, I mumbled, "Showtime," which now had an entirely new meaning. But little did I know that showtime had only begun.

11:20 P.M.
City Hall—Dallas

Buell Frazier, the Depository employee who had driven Oswald to work on the morning of the assassination, is arrested and brought in for questioning. His rifle, a British 303 Enfield with a fully loaded clip, is confiscated. He receives, and passes, a polygraph examination.

Oswald is removed from his cell and taken to the show-up room for the fourth time. On this occasion he is brought before the news media for a press conference.

Jack Ruby has arrived at City Hall from Nichol's Parking Garage and his strange escapade of having the attendant date and time stamp Little Lynn's five-dollar receipt. (In retrospect, this action is an apparent attempt to establish an alibi that will support a lack of premeditation had he been able to murder Oswald at this time. This action is almost an exact duplication of his episode at the Western Union Office on the following morning just before he kills Oswald.)

Through his ownership of the Carousel Club, Ruby is friends with many of the Dallas police officers. This friendship allows him access to areas that are off-limits to other citizens. Now in attendance for Oswald's press conference, he stands on a table at the rear of the show-up room *with a loaded pistol in his pocket*.

Following a brief question and answer session with reporters, Oswald is taken back to his cell. District Attorney Henry Wade remains behind and outlines Oswald's activities and background to the reporters. While doing so, he erroneously states that Oswald was a member of the "Free Cuba Committee." He is quickly corrected by Ruby. From his position at the back of the room, Ruby tells Wade that he means "Fair Play for Cuba Committee." Only a person very familiar with Cuban politics of that period would know the difference between the Free Cuba Committee, an *anti*-Castro organization, and the Fair Play for Cuba Committee, a *pro*-Castro network. Ruby's close affiliation with Cuba-connected mobsters, as well as his Cuban gunrunning activities, made him knowledgeable of these politically-opposite organizations.

11:26 P.M.

Chief Curry and Dallas District Attorney
Henry Wade decide to file charges against
Oswald for the murder of the President. Cap-
tain Fritz signs the complaint and gives it to
Wade and his assistant Bill Alexander.

DAY TWO—
SATURDAY—
NOVEMBER 23, 1963

12:10 A.M.

City Jail—Dallas

For apparently the fifth time Oswald is taken to the first floor show-up room. On this occasion he is accompanied by all the detectives in the Homicide and Robbery division as well as numerous other detectives and uniformed officers. He remains there only five minutes. No explanation or reason is given for this action. Was this used as an opportunity to "bug" or search his cell? Or both? He is then taken by elevator to the fourth-floor jail for searching (his third) and booking.

12:20 A.M.

Oswald is taken to the fifth-floor jail and placed in a cell for the night.

1:35 A.M.

According to police reports, Lee Harvey Oswald is arraigned for the murder of President John F. Kennedy before Justice of the Peace David Johnston. Hours earlier, a complaint against Oswald for the murder of Officer Tippit was processed. Formal arraignment followed just minutes later. In the case of the President's murder, however, formal arraignment does not occur until two hours after the complaint was signed. There is considerable doubt whether he was actually arraigned at all.

If Oswald was arraigned at 1:35 A.M., what was the reason for this long delay? And why was he taken from his cell in the middle of the night? Normal procedure would be to hold the arraignment when court opened on Monday. Of course, Oswald would have been dead by then and Dallas authorities made to look even more inept, their suspect deceased prior to formal charges being filed.

Perhaps Oswald's midnight press conference can shed some light on this puzzle. At that time Oswald was asked by a reporter, "Did you kill the President?" Oswald replied, "I have not been charged with that. *In fact nobody has said that to me yet*. The first thing I heard about it was when the newspaper reporters in the hall asked me that question."

Is Oswald feigning ignorance, or had he truly not been informed of his being a suspect in the President's murder?

Dallas police attempted to leave no doubt that they had quickly and efficiently solved the case and that Oswald had been arraigned for President Kennedy's murder. This self-serving effort is categorically disputed by an FBI document that states, "No arraignment of the murder charges in connection with the death of President Kennedy was held inasmuch as such arraignment was not necessary in view of the previous charges filed against Oswald and for which he was arraigned."

3:40 A.M.

White House—Washington, D.C.

The President's body finally arrives at the White House and is taken to the East Room. The original time of arrival had been 10:00 P.M., some nine and one-half hours after the assassination. The scheduled arrival had been moved to 11:00, then 12:00, then 1:00 A.M., then 2:00, then 3:00, before finally reaching the White House at 3:40 A.M. It has been fifteen hours since the shots rang out in Dallas.

Queried about the delay, the slain President's chief physician, Dr. George Burkley, responds, "It's taking longer than expected." He was not asked, nor did he offer, to explain what "It" was.

Jacqueline Kennedy accompanies the President's flag-draped casket into the East Room. She is still wearing her bloodstained pink suit, though she has been urged by several people on several occasions to change. She had replied, "No! I want THEM to see what THEY have done."

7:30 A.M.

Oswald awakens to eat breakfast and to resume questioning by various authorities.

Parkland Hospital—Dallas

"What is your name, sir?" a deep, polite voice boomed from the tall policeman.

"Dr. Charles Crenshaw," I replied. "I'm a surgeon at this hospital."

As I reached into my pocket to produce identification, Parkland's assistant administrator, who was standing beside the officer, nodded at him in confirmation, and I was allowed to pass. When I walked through the doorway, the scene in the hallway verified what I had suspected as I had driven into Parkland's parking lot—that it was to be another unusual day.

Automobiles bearing the markings of news organizations, law enforcement departments, and state and federal agencies were everywhere, as were the officials, roaming between the hospital and the medical school, vigilantly patrolling the area. Still looming in the minds of the police was the concern of a conspiracy to kill Governor Connally.

Newsmen were frantically perusing the premises for an interview with anyone wearing a white coat. Police worried about security. Medical personnel were trying to provide health care. And the men in suits were still lurking about, cultivating an aura of trepidation and intimidation. They always had the "game face" look of being perpetually pissed off.

"Dr. Crenshaw, tell me about the procedures that you performed on the President," a reporter asked, intentionally blocking my path toward the emergency room. Apparently, the news media had identified every doctor who had been in Trauma Room 1, and we were being searched out for interviews.

"Did he say anything before he died?" another reporter immediately asked.

"How many times was he shot?" someone else shouted, while more newsmen gathered around me.

"What is the condition of Governor Connally?" a voice demanded to know.

"Do you believe Oswald shot Kennedy in the back of the head from the Texas School Book Depository Building?" a man with CBS inquired as the cameraman behind him shone lights in my eyes.

The question shocked me. Instantly, a scenario began to form in my mind, and the thought was terrifying. If Lee Harvey Oswald was the lone assassin, they have a lunatic, a madman. But if I tell them the medical truth, that President Kennedy was shot from the front, they have more than one gunman, they have a conspiracy, I thought to myself.

Then I remembered Agent Hill waving his pistol in Trauma Room 1, and how the men in suits had moved the President's body out of Parkland before an autopsy could be performed—how they would have shot Earl Rose and anyone else who had gotten in their way—how the President's limousine had been rushed out of view when the bullet hole in the windshield was noticed by the medical student. The people involved in this game played for keeps. For the first time, I sensed the presence of the pervasive influence of corruption, and it chilled me to the bone.

Just as the film was about to roll, I replied, "An official statement was made yesterday. I have nothing to add. Now, if you would excuse me." With that, I turned and threaded my way through the crowd of people toward the emergency room. At that moment I entered the "conspiracy of silence." I wasn't asked or told to do so, nor was any overt pressure ever placed upon me. I was acting from an instinctive survival feeling, the one that had gotten me through medical school, through internship, and into one of the best surgical residency programs in the country. To do otherwise would have meant saying, "Hell, no, Oswald didn't shoot him

in the head, because the President was shot from the front." None of us doctors were willing to do that. We all valued our medical careers too much.

At a news conference in the hospital the previous day, Drs. Malcolm Perry and Kemp Clark suggested that the President must have been turning to his right when he was shot. They said this because they also believed that the bullet that ripped through President Kennedy's head had entered from the front. When the films showed that the President was not turned when he was shot, nothing more was said, as I remember. I didn't blame Drs. Clark and Perry one bit. They, too, had observed the men in suits, and had heard about the scene with Dr. Earl Rose. Every doctor who was in Trauma Room 1 had his own reasons for not publicly refuting the "official line."

I believe there was a common denominator in our silence—a fearful perception that to come forward with what we believed to be the medical truth would be asking for trouble. Although we never admitted it to one another, we realized that the inertia of the established story was so powerful, so thoroughly presented, so adamantly accepted, that it would bury anyone who stood in its path. I had already witnessed that awesome, dictatorial force in the Earl Rose incident, the same fierceness that I would, for years to come, continue to recognize in the tragedies awaiting those people who sought the truth. I was as afraid of the men in suits as I was of the men who had assassinated the President. Whatever was happening was larger than any of us. I reasoned that anyone who would go so far

as to eliminate the President of the United States would surely not hesitate to kill a doctor.

It wasn't that we doctors had an interest in disputing the one rifle, one man, one assassin theory. We're physicians, not police investigators, and detective work is not our business. But in this case, the medical evidence I saw overwhelmingly disputed the Warren Commission's claim as to the direction from which two of the bullets came that struck the President.

Dr. J. J. Humes, the physician who performed the autopsy at Bethesda, called Dr. Perry, inquiring about the President's neck wound. Until informed, Dr. Humes was not aware that a bullet had entered the President's throat—only that a tracheostomy had been performed at that spot. After that discussion, we questioned the ability and qualifications of the team that performed the autopsy on the President. We heard reports that those doctors hadn't conducted an autopsy for years. And when I recently saw the official autopsy pictures, I knew something had been askew. If a postmortem examination had been conducted on President Kennedy at Parkland, more questions would have been raised and the autopsy pictures would have told a different story, one that would have led the investigation in other directions.

I've often wondered what would have been the consequences of looking directly into that camera and boldly stating, "President Kennedy was shot in the head and in the throat from the front." Now, after all these years, I realize that such courage would have been utterly ineffective and suicidal.

The truth, staring directly into the face of our government, stood about as much chance of coming to light as a june bug in a hailstorm, and I wouldn't have fared any better.

Already, the eastern press had begun to discredit us as physicians and Parkland as a hospital. If you had any association with Dallas, you were suspect. To come forward and give an unwavering professional opinion that was contradictory to the official story would only have given them a personalized target. I never understood why the government didn't behave in the same manner, why the press wasn't equally critical, or why the American people didn't condemn Los Angeles when Robert Kennedy was killed as they had Dallas when President Kennedy was assassinated.

The hospital administration was paranoid about publicity, especially at a time like that. In view of all I had heard, seen, and sensed, I wasn't about to appear on the six-o'clock news, giving an interview about the death of the President. A nursing student had already fallen into disfavor, and was later thrown out of school, because she informed the press of the number of blood units Governor Connally had received.

Although no official instructions had been issued by the hospital administration, there was a tacit implication, an unspoken warning in their general attitudes that said that anyone who was intelligent enough to pursue a medical career was also smart enough to keep his mouth shut. Failure to do the latter would result in foreclosure on the former. We were all young doctors who for years had struggled and sacrificed to achieve that level of success. And we had a fortune in money and time tied up in our professions. The thought of throwing all that away weighed heavily on my mind.

Avoiding several more reporters, I rushed through the emergency room, past the Obstetrics and Gynecological section, and entered the stairwell that Dr. McClelland and I had descended the previous day on our way to Trauma Room 1. I was anxious to see how Connally's blood work looked since midnight, and I still had other patients to care for. Newsmen were even camped out on the stairs, waiting for doctors to pass. Two of them followed me up to the second floor.

The scene in the surgical suite was equally chaotic. A Texas Ranger wearing boots and a ten-gallon hat was stationed in the hall just outside the anesthesia call room. He looked eight feet tall. One riot—one Ranger—that was their reputation. Again, I was identified and allowed to pass. I immediately went into the doctors' dressing room and changed my clothes. But looking like doctors didn't exclude us from having to clear every security checkpoint as we moved about the hospital.

Several minutes later, Dr. Shires and I went in to see Governor Connally. His wife was still inside the makeshift, intensive care area. Drs. Shaw and Duke had seen Connally earlier that morning. They had checked his chest tube to make sure his lung was not collapsing. The governor was also made to cough, to expand his lungs and prevent pneumonia, which was extremely painful because of his shattered rib.

Usually, the chief of surgery observes while the resident changes a dressing. But Dr. Shires did it for Connally, and I thought that was appropriate. If I were the governor, I would expect that level of care. Governor Connally was alert and seemed to be doing well. Each day, he was moved to a different room within ward 2-East to prevent another attempt on his life from a window. But nothing ever happened at Parkland that indicated anyone wanted to harm him. Apparently, his only misfortune had been catching a stray bullet while riding in the same limousine with a man marked for death.

After I looked in on the rest of my patients, I went into the doctors' lounge. Many of the physicians in there were drinking coffee and talking about the assassination. Down the hall, other doctors were watching as the networks continued to condemn Dallas on television. Everyone was melancholy, in slow motion, still in shock. Parkland had lost the most important patient it would ever have, and Dallas had earned a dubious place in history.

10:30 A.M.

City Hall—Dallas

Oswald is removed from his cell and taken to Captain Fritz's office for his second of five official interrogations. Also present, in addition to Fritz and other homicide officers, were Secret Service Agents Forrest Sorrels and James Bookhout as well as U.S. Marshal Robert Nash.

11:30 A.M.
City Hall—Dallas

Detectives Elmer Boyd, C. N. Dhority, and Ray Hall obtain a search warrant from Justice of the Peace Joe B. Brown, Jr., for Oswald's rooming house. They proceed to the residence and again search Oswald's room.

11:33 A.M.

The second interrogation complete, Oswald is returned to his cell.

12:30 P.M.

Detectives Gus Rose, Richard Stovall, John Adamcik, and Elmer Moore obtain a search warrant from Justice of the Peace Joe B. Brown, Jr., for the home of Michael and Ruth Paine at 2515 West Fifth Street in Irving. Marina Oswald and the two children have been residing with the Paines since moving from New Orleans. Oswald had spent the previous Thursday night in their home visiting his family. After her husband's arrest, Marina and the children were whisked away into protective custody by the FBI. First, they were sequestered in the Hotel Adolphus, then in the Executive Inn Motel, and finally in the Inn of Six Flags in nearby Arlington. They were not present for this search. The officers seized several articles belonging to Oswald.

12:35 P.M.

Oswald is brought back to Captain Fritz's office for the third interrogation since his arrest. FBI Agent Bookhout and Secret Service Agent Kelly are present as are homicide officers and a man named George Carlston. For the first time Oswald is shown a small snapshot of the soon to become famous photograph of himself holding a rifle, Communist newspapers, and with a revolver on his hip. He had no comment.

1:10 P.M.

The interrogation of Oswald is halted and he is taken back to his cell. His wife Marina and mother Marguerite visit him for twenty minutes.

2:15 P.M.

For the final time Oswald is taken downstairs to the show-up room. On this occasion two taxi drivers, William Whaley and W. W. Scoggins, identify Oswald. Scoggins says that Oswald is the man he saw running from the scene of the shooting of Officer Tippit. Whaley claims Oswald was the passenger he drove from downtown Dallas to Oak Cliff following the assassination of President Kennedy.

3:30 P.M.

Oswald's brother, Robert, arrives at the jail and visits him for five minutes.

3:30 P.M.

County Records Building—Dallas

District Attorney Henry Wade continues working on the Oswald case.

Parkland Hospital—Dallas

With only three hours' sleep since Friday morning, I felt exhausted. So, I was lying down in the residents' call room, dozing. It was the lightest day I could ever remember having at Parkland. The whole city was in shock over the President's death. For the moment, people had quit drinking, stabbing, and shooting.

Just as I was beginning to enter a deeper sleep, the telephone rang. It was the emergency room requesting a doctor come down to examine a man who appeared to be having an attack of appendicitis. The trauma team was in surgery, so they called me because I was in charge of elective surgery "B." I sent a first-year resident down to examine the patient. In a few minutes the resident called me to report that he believed the man needed to be taken to surgery for an appendectomy. I struggled out of bed and trudged down to the emergency room.

The patient was having abdominal pain, but I wasn't convinced that he needed surgery. I decided to observe him for several hours and let his body tell us what to do. Many times at private hospitals, the procedure is to first get the patient comfortable by giving him a pain shot—that's what he's paying for, and that's what he expects. But at an academic hospital, we allow the patient to endure a reasonable amount of pain if it's necessary to give us an accurate diagnosis. Pain medication camouflages symptoms, which can waste valuable time and result in incorrect medical treatment, both of which are dangerous to the patient.

6:00 P.M.

City Hall—Dallas

Captain Fritz holds the fourth interrogation of Oswald in his office. Present for this interview are other homicide officers, Secret Service Agent Kelly, and FBI Agent Bookhout. On this occasion Oswald is shown an enlargement of the photograph of himself holding the guns. This time he repudiates its authenticity, declaring that the "face is mine," but the body was not, and the photo was a composite. He understood photography real well, he said, and in time he would be able to show that it was not his picture.

7:15 P.M.

Oswald is returned to his cell.

9:30 P.M.

Michael Paine gives Detectives John Adamcik and Elmer Moore an affidavit saying he had observed a rifle wrapped in a blanket in his garage on a few occasions prior to the assassination.

Parkland Hospital—Dallas

It took at least five rings for the telephone to penetrate the heavy state of sleep that had gripped me. As I struggled to find my ear with the receiver, I stepped out of my dream and back into Parkland.

"Dr. Crenshaw, I would appreciate your coming down and reexamining the patient with the abdominal pain," came the resident's voice from the black plastic pressed to my head. "His temperature is beginning to rise."

"I'll be right there," I uttered lethargically.

Once on my feet, I ran my hands through my hair and splashed some cold water on my face. When I walked from the residents' call room and into the hall, I saw people wandering around as if they were at an amusement park. Parkland was still in shock and moving in slow motion, just as I was. The hospital remained abuzz with talk about Kennedy. Members of the press continued to roam the halls, looking for interviews and stories.

On my way to the observation area in the emergency room, I stopped in to see Governor Connally to make sure he was comfortable and to check the dressing on his leg. As a security measure, all the rooms in ward 2-E had been vacated.

My patient in the emergency room was still having pain in his right lower quadrant, had a slight temperature, and his white count was increasing but was not yet in the dangerous range. It was still too early to determine if he needed surgery. Many times, patients with these symptoms will suddenly improve without further treatment. If he was having an attack of appendicitis, the signals from his body were not conclusive. Being in pain is not in itself a sufficient reason to cut open the abdomen. First, I must have a confirmed diagnosis.

Before I went back to the second floor, I walked around the emergency room, marveling at the small number of people who were being treated. With so few cases, the chances of getting a good night's sleep were excellent. The President's death had almost brought Dallas to a complete halt.

On my way back to the residents' call room, I took a quick detour into the anesthesia call room and again saw Oswald on television. A reporter was speculating that President Kennedy had been shot three times by Oswald from the Texas School Book Depository Building, and that one of the bullets had gone through Kennedy's body and then hit Governor Connally. When I heard that, I looked at Dr. "Red" Duke and shook my head in amazement. He returned the gesture. Again, I thought of the opening in the President's throat that was an entry wound. Later, when the magic bullet theory was propagated by the Warren Commission, I immediately concluded that no bullet would have had the energy to go through that much tissue, cartilage, muscle, and bone of two men, and remain intact. Plus, I had seen the bullet fragments taken from Governor Connally's wrist. We knew that theory was ridiculous. But that was the story that was being disseminated. It later became the official story.

11:00 P.M.
City Hall—Dallas

Dallas Homicide Captain Will Fritz receives a person-to-person telephone call from new President Lyndon Johnson. He is *ordered* to stop his investigation. Fritz had been attempting to conduct a thorough investigation into the President's murder despite interference and opposition from federal authorities. He had received several phone calls urging him to cease the investigation because, "You have your man." Fritz had thus far ignored these cajolings and had continued his investigation. He halted the inquiry only after receiving the President's order. (Years later, reflecting back, Fritz tells close friends, "But when the President of the United States called . . . what could I do?")

11:44 P.M.
Downtown Dallas

Jack Ruby leaves his Carousel Club and goes to the Pago Club to visit a friend.

Parkland Hospital—Dallas

I called down to the emergency room to get a report on my patient. The resident informed me that he was asleep, and that his temperature was the same as the last time we had checked. I told him that unless our patient's condition worsened, if he didn't need surgery by nine o'clock in the morning, elective surgery "C" would be on duty and they could take over his case.

DAY THREE— SUNDAY— NOVEMBER 24, 1963

2:15 A.M.

Sheriff's Office—Dallas

Sheriff's Officer Perry McCoy receives a phone call from a "white male" who tells McCoy that Oswald is going to be killed during his transfer from the city jail to the county jail. The reason for calling, McCoy is told, is that the caller wants the department to have the information so that none of the deputies would get hurt.

2:20 A.M.

City Hall—Dallas

Police Lieutenant Billy Grammer, working in the communications room, also receives a message from an unidentified caller. The caller specifically asks to speak with Grammer after inquiring of another officer as to who is on duty. Refusing to identify himself, the man tells Grammer, "You know me." He then begins to describe the plans for Oswald's transfer in detail and tells the lieutenant that other arrangements should be made or, "We're going to kill Oswald right there in the basement." The voice of the caller is familiar to Grammer, but he is unable to put a face to it. The threat is taken seriously and a report is filed with Chief Curry.

2:30 A.M.

FBI Office—Dallas

An unnamed employee of the local FBI office receives a telephone call from an anonymous male. Speaking in a calm and mature voice, the caller advises that he represented "A committee . . . we are going to kill the man who killed the President."

3:20 A.M.

City Hall—Dallas

Dallas Police Captain W. B. Frazier receives a call from FBI Agent Milton Newsom informing him that an anonymous threat to kill Oswald was received at the Dallas FBI office.

Parkland Hospital—Dallas

All was quiet at Parkland Hospital, and I was getting some much needed sleep.

6:00 A.M.

Parkland Hospital—Dallas

I awakened at six o'clock that Sunday morning, feeling rested, a sensation that seldom came my way. For a resident surgeon, getting six hours of uninterrupted sleep ranks up there with a raise in salary.

The reporters had already returned to Parkland, and security was still tight. And of course, the ever-present men in suits were still there. I put on a fresh scrub suit and went down to the emergency room to check on my patient. I saw no real change in his condition.

I rushed to the cafeteria and ate breakfast, then returned to the second floor to see more of my patients and meet Dr. Shires to check on the governor's condition. He was still being moved from room to room, and protective devices were placed in front of all windows to prevent snipers from shooting into the room.

6:30 A.M.
City Jail—Dallas

Captain Fritz arrives at City Hall in preparation for further questioning of Oswald.

7:00 A.M.

The Dallas police begin preparations for transferring Oswald out of the Dallas city jail. The basement is cleared and guards are stationed at the ramps leading into the garage.

9:00 A.M.

Chicago

An officer of the Chicago branch of the American Guild of Variety Artists (AGVA) sends a message intended for Jack Ruby in Dallas. The message reads, "Tell Jack not to send the letter today, it would be awkward in Chicago." AGVA is an entertainers' union long dominated by members of organized crime. Coded language is a common tool of the underworld, and the meaning of this cryptic order has never been adequately explained or investigated. Whatever its meaning, the orders were never delivered to Ruby.

9:30 A.M.

City Jail—Dallas

At the Dallas Police Department, James R. Leavelle, a homicide detective, recommends to Dallas Police Chief Curry that additional precautions be taken by making Oswald's transfer on the first floor, rather than the basement; that double-crossing the news media will create an effective diversion. Curry

tells Leavelle that the television people will
be allowed to document the transfer of Oswald to show that he has not been abused
or beaten.

Detectives Leavelle and L. C. Graves are
told that they will transfer Oswald to the Dallas County jail. They then remove Oswald
from his jail cell and take him to Captain
Fritz's third-floor office for further questioning. Present are Captain Fritz, several
homicide detectives, Secret Service Agents Forrest Sorrells and Thomas Kelly, and U.S.
Postal Inspector Harry Holmes. Chief Curry
sits in briefly at the beginning of the interrogation.

Minister Ray Rushing arrives at City Hall
and takes the elevator to the third floor.
While on the elevator, Rushing meets and
talks with Jack Ruby. The minister is one of
four witnesses who testified that they had
seen Ruby in or near the police building at
various times between 8:00 A.M. and 11:00
A.M.

Parkland Hospital—Dallas

Officially, my surgical team was off duty, and
elective "C" had begun. I had finished making
rounds to see all my patients, including the man in
the observation room with the abdominal pain, who

I had just turned over to elective "C." We were in the doctors' lounge, drinking coffee and smoking cigarettes. Depending upon one's rank, a doctor often had to stand while his superiors occupied the limited seating. As a third-year resident, I was sitting that morning, along with Drs. Shires, Perry, Jones, and Duke.

Had I not gotten so much sleep the previous night, I would have gone home. But feeling rested, I stayed to talk with my colleagues about the assassination and how Parkland had been taken over by law enforcement officials and the news media. With an air of suspicion and excitement hovering over the hospital, none of us wanted to leave. We felt that Parkland was under siege, and we wanted to protect it. I don't believe Dr. "Red" Duke left the hospital for three days. It was almost as if we sensed that something else would happen, and we residents didn't want to miss it. At that point, nothing would have surprised us.

Also high on the discussion list was Kennedy's autopsy at Bethesda. After Dr. Perry's conversation with J. J. Humes, the doctor who conducted the postmortem examination, we had doubts as to whether they were qualified to conduct an autopsy of this nature. And, although carefully and quietly stated, we were expressing the same views on the direction from which the bullets had been fired that struck President Kennedy and Governor Connally. We never knew that the men in suits might be listening.

10:35 A.M.

Dallas—City Hall

Ira Walker, WBAP (Fort Worth) television technician, is inside the station's news van at the audio board awaiting Oswald's transfer. The van is located just outside City Hall. Jack Ruby comes up to the window and asks Walker, "Has he (Oswald) been brought down yet?"

11:00 A.M.

Dallas

The Reverend William A. Holmes, pastor of the Northaven United Methodist Church, delivers a sermon critical of Dallas. He poignantly states, "President John Kennedy was killed two days ago in Dallas, and the one thing worse than this is that the citizens of Dallas should declare unto the world, 'We take no responsibility for the death of this man' . . . There is no city in the United States which in recent months and years has been more acquiescent toward its extremists than Dallas, Texas."

After Holmes's discourse was broadcast on "The CBS Evening News" two days later, he receives telephone calls that threaten his life. Agents advise him that he should leave Dallas for several days.

Parkland Hospital—Dallas

Parkland Hospital officials are notified by Bob Struwe, the hospital controller, that large crowds have gathered to watch Oswald's transfer.

Before leaving his cell for the basement, Oswald puts on a black sweater to disguise himself since everyone has seen him on television in his clothes. He turns to Leavelle and says, "There ain't nobody gonna shoot me."

11:17 A.M.
City Hall—Dallas

Jack Ruby leaves City Hall, walks a half-block to the Western Union Office, and sends a $25.00 money order to Little Lynn, one of his strippers, in Fort Worth. The timing of this transaction, in light of his appearance and disappearance at the Dallas Morning News Building at the time of the President's shooting, seems to be another alibi-producing maneuver. It eventually served to establish Ruby's lack of premeditation for Oswald's murder. In reality, since the announced transfer time was 10:00 A.M., it also appears likely that Ruby possessed inside knowledge of when Oswald would be moved.

Upon returning the short distance to City Hall, Ruby enters through an unguarded door, proceeds down one flight of stairs to the basement, crosses the parking area, and joins the group of policemen and reporters awaiting Oswald's transfer. His timing could not have been more perfect. As if on cue, Oswald, handcuffed to Detectives Leavelle and Graves, enters the basement area from the adjoining jail office. As an unmarked car backs into position to pick up Oswald and transport him to the county jail a few blocks away, the sound of a car honking echoes through the basement. As Oswald nears Ruby's position he appears to glance quickly toward him, then turn away.

Detective Leavelle, cuffed to Oswald's right arm, notices Ruby holding a pistol by his side. He sees Ruby crouch, extend the pistol, and quickly move in on his prisoner, but he has no time to react. Ruby, gripping a .38 Colt Cobra pistol tightly in his right hand in an "assassin's grip" (a Chicago term for the grip used by an assassin to prevent the weapon from being wrenched from his hand; this grip utilizes the middle finger on the trigger and the index finger on the cylinder above), he fires one shot point-blank into Oswald's left midsection. Oswald cries out loudly in pain and collapses to the floor.

Detective Graves, escorting Oswald by his left arm, catches only a glimpse of Ruby passing in front of him to deliver the fatal shot. Grasping Ruby's wrist and gun simultaneously, he spins around with the assailant while other officers converge to assist. Together the officers subdue Ruby and wrest the weapon from his hand. In the midst of the struggle Ruby blurts out, "You all know me, I'm Jack Ruby."

Standing nearby, Detective Don Archer witnesses the shooting and assists in apprehending Ruby. He and other officers place Ruby in a fifth-floor cell. Archer, staying behind to guard the prisoner, observes Ruby's strange behavior. Ruby was "very hyper" and "sweating profusely." He had been stripped down for security purposes and his rapid heartbeat could readily be seen. Ruby requested and was given a cigarette. Later, word came that Oswald had died as a result of the shooting. Archer conveys this information to Ruby, telling him that, "It looks like it's going to be the electric chair for you.'' Instead of becoming more agitated, Ruby became calm, ceased perspiring, and his rapid heartbeat slowed to normal. Archer then asks Ruby if he would like another cigarette. Ruby replied, "I don't smoke." Ruby's behavior, Archer noted, was a "complete turnaround." It was apparent that his life depended on his getting Oswald.

Parkland Hospital—Dallas

The first-year resident on my surgical service called me from the emergency room, advising that the patient with the apparent appendicitis could wait no longer for an appendectomy, that his temperature and white count had increased considerably during the past hour. I told him that if Jones would staff "C" service, and would allow him to operate, I had no objections. Several minutes later, they were in surgery. Like most first- and second-year surgical residents, he was hungry for action.

11:21 A.M.
City Hall—Dallas

Detectives Leavelle and Billy Combest carry Oswald back inside the jail. Fred Bieberdorf, a medical student and city jail medical attendant who is in the basement, gives a cardiac massage when no heartbeat is detected.

Parkland Hospital—Dallas

Elective surgery "C" was operating on the appendectomy patient, and the trauma team was also in surgery. Dr. Shires had just left the hospital, and I was still sitting in the doctors' lounge, talking with Dr. Perry. The telephone rang, and I answered it. On the other end of the line was the hospital administrator C. J. (Jack) Price. When I identified myself, he asked me who had a free operating team. I told him that there were no available surgical services, that the one that had just come on was in surgery. In a strained voice, he imparted to me that he needed an operating team down in the emergency room immediately. I had never known the hospital administrator to call the doctors' lounge and request a surgical team, especially in such an anxious voice. So I agreed, and took what was left of surgical service "B," and Drs. Gerry Gustafson and Dale Coln, both residents, and went downstairs. Dr. Perry and the others remained in the doctors' lounge. At that point, none of us knew that Oswald was on his way to Parkland.

11:24 A.M.
City Hall—Dallas

The ambulance arrives at the jail. Oswald is thrown onto a gurney and shoved into the back of the vehicle. Bieberdorf accompanies Oswald to Parkland, giving heart massage the entire way.

Jack Ruby is taken upstairs at the city jail for interrogation. He reveals that it was his intention to shoot Oswald three times.

Parkland Hospital—Dallas

We were standing in the hallway, just outside Trauma Room 1 when Jack Price told us that Lee Harvey Oswald had been shot and was en route to Parkland. I simply could not believe that we were about to treat the alleged assassin of President Kennedy.

I noticed that several nurses were readying Trauma Room 1. In perhaps the most perceptive moment of my life, I turned to a nurse and exclaimed, "In deference to President Kennedy, we will not treat this patient in Trauma Room 1. When Oswald arrives, put him in Trauma Room 2." At that time we all assumed that Oswald was the killer of our President.

Price's face lit up in agreement. Immediately, he

recognized the long-term significance of that decision. For years, Jack Price has repeatedly expressed to me his appreciation that I had had the presence of mind to make that distinction.

Word of Oswald's impending arrival traveled the hospital halls faster than a staph infection. Dr. Ronald Jones was called out of surgery. He rushed down to join me and the rest of our group while we waited for the ambulance to arrive. Dr. Perry remained on the second floor to assemble a surgical team while the operating room was being readied. Having seen the shooting on television, Dr. McClelland rushed out of his Highland Park home and drove to the hospital. And when Dr. Shires heard the news on his radio, he turned his car around and headed back toward Parkland.

11:30 A.M.

Dallas

Dallas Police Lieutenant Billy Grammer is at home asleep after his night-shift duty at police headquarters. He is suddenly awakened by his wife who tells him that a man named Jack Ruby has just shot Lee Harvey Oswald while in the basement of the police station. Only now does a face appear to go with that familiar voice who called earlier, while he was on duty, to warn of Oswald's impending death. He also recalled having unexpectedly met, and talked with Ruby in a restaurant near the station only a week before. This recollection served to cement his identification of the voice on the phone as being that of Ruby.

11:32 A.M.

Parkland Hospital—Dallas

Lee Harvey Oswald is wheeled into the emergency room at Parkland Hospital.

As Oswald was rolled into Trauma Room 2, he was deathly pale. I observed that he had dilated pupils, was unconscious and unresponsive, had no palpable pulse, but did have a heartbeat. The bullet had entered his left thorax, traveled through his body, and could be felt just under the skin on his right side. From his bloated abdomen, it was evident that his injury was causing him to continue to lose blood internally.

We quickly cut away Oswald's clothing, underwear and all. Then, while Dr. Jenkins inserted the endotracheal tube, Drs. Coln, Gustafson, and I performed three venous cutdowns, one on each leg and one on the left forearm. I did the one on the right ankle. Without delay, we initiated Ringer's lactate, then got "O" negative blood flowing into two cutdowns. In violation of hospital policy, but as a measure he believed he had to take if Oswald was to have a chance of surviving, Dr. "Red" Duke had sprinted to the blood bank and collected an armful of "O" negative blood, and returned to the emergency room without documenting the withdrawal. "O" negative blood is a universal type, and can be given to anyone. I believe that demonstrated the effort we all made to save the man.

Simultaneously, Jones inserted a chest tube and connected it to a closed waterseal drainage bottle to prevent Oswald's left lung from collapsing. A blood sample was sent to the blood bank for immediate typing, the front of the gurney was lowered to help get blood to his heart and brain, and Dr. Risk catheterized him. In record time, only seven and one-half minutes, we had completed the resuscitation procedure and had him on his way to surgery. We all sensed the significance of saving Oswald.

Getting him up to surgery was like a fire drill. At least a dozen of us, entangled in tubes and equipment, pushed the gurney, plus IV stands and an anesthesia machine down the hall and squeezed into a small elevator. On our way up to surgery, we suddenly stopped on the first floor. As the doors opened, two of Oswald's friends, who were on their way to the emergency room, came into full view. They never knew it was Lee Harvey lying on that cart, because all they saw was a mass of humanity and equipment.

Once on the second floor, we rushed Oswald into the operating room. Drs. McClelland and Shires had not yet arrived, but did so just minutes after the operation began. As we prepared to open Oswald's abdomen, Dr. Duke arrived with a pasteboard box full of type-correct blood units (A-1 Rh negative), which were administered under pressure through the three cutdowns.

I will never forget "Red" Duke continuously circling the operating table, carrying that box of blood. Around and around he went, IV pole to IV pole, replacing empty bottles with full ones, while tube bulbs were being squeezed to increase the volume of fluids going into Oswald's circulatory system. If we hadn't had large amounts of blood entering him through the cutdown veins before his abdomen was exposed, his remaining blood volume would have quickly emptied when the incision was made, and he would have bled to death in only seconds.

At 11:44 A.M., twelve minutes after Oswald had been admitted to Parkland, Dr. Perry made a midline abdominal incision that began just below the sternum and extended almost to his pubis. When the peritoneum (an envelope-like lining in the abdomen) was cut, three liters of liquid and clotted blood, three-fourths of Oswald's volume (almost one gallon) gushed from his abdomen like water from a bursting balloon. It went everywhere—on the sheets, on the floor, on us. When the pressure in the abdomen was released, the remaining blood in Oswald's body began rushing into his abdomen through numerous portals.

As I held a retractor with one hand, and suctioned blood from the abdominal cavity with the other hand, Dr. Shires assessed the internal injuries. In a split second, a piece of lead smaller than a thimble had done no less harm to Oswald's abdomen than would several blows with an ax. The bullet had lacerated the aorta and vena cava (which is the large vein running from the abdomen to the heart), shattered the spleen, and slashed through the stomach, pancreas, kidney, liver, and finally lodged in the right lateral body wall. It did about as much damage to the vital organs as one shot can do.

Blood was running and squirting into the abdomen through each of the wounds, especially the spleen, aorta, and the vena cava. Drs. Shires, McClelland, Perry, and Jones were attaching clamps and applying finger pressure to the arteries, veins, and organs to stop the bleeding before they could begin repairing the damage. The scene that day was equivalent to preventing a boat from sinking when it's taking on water, with part of the crew bailing and the others plugging holes.

After the major bleeding had been brought under control, I looked up and took a deep breath. When I did, I spotted a large man across the room whom I didn't recognize. He resembled Oliver Hardy in a scrub suit with no mask. Most alarming, there was a pistol hanging from his back pocket; if it had fallen to the floor, it could have discharged and killed someone. I never knew how he got into the operating room or who gave him the scrub suit.

Just two days earlier, a Secret Service agent had rushed through the emergency room, waving a gun as the President of the United States lay there, dying. Incredibly, the man who had been accused of shooting President Kennedy was now lying before me, fighting for his life, while another pistol-packing intruder looked on. I didn't know what to think, except that we had to get a cap and mask on the son of a bitch before he contaminated the entire room with bacteria.

I motioned for one of the other resident surgeons to relieve me. I scrubbed out and got the proper attire for the guy. I wanted to throw his ass out of the operating room, but I was afraid he would shoot me. Without saying anything, I handed him the cap and mask. He put it on without comment. As I was turning around, a nurse tapped me on the shoulder and asked if I would take a telephone call in the supervisor's office. She had chosen me to take the call because I was the head of Surgical "B," the team that began the operation. I agreed to answer the call and left the operating room. When I entered the office, the receiver was lying on the desk.

"This is Dr. Crenshaw, may I help you?"

"This is President Lyndon B. Johnson," the voice thundered. "Dr. Crenshaw, how is the accused assassin?"

I couldn't believe what I was hearing. The very first thought that I had was, how did he know when to call?

"Mr. President, he's holding his own at the moment," I reported.

"Would you mind taking a message to the operating surgeon?" he asked in a manner that sounded more like an order.

"Dr. Shires is very busy right now, but I will convey your message."

"Dr. Crenshaw, I want a deathbed confession from the accused assassin. There's a man in the operating room who will take the statement. I will expect full cooperation in this matter," he said firmly.

"Yes, sir," I replied and hung up the telephone. I almost laughed in the President's ear. If he could have seen the mess in the operating room and the condition of our patient, he wouldn't have asked.

As I stood there in a state of disbelief, my mind was racing. First, "deathbed confession" implies that someone is going to die. If Oswald doesn't die on the table, is "Oliver Hardy" or someone else going to kill him?

Second, anyone who knows anything about Texas politics is familiar with the 1948 U.S. Senate race when Johnson defeated Coke Stevenson, and the election improprieties that were documented in South Texas. It occurred to me that if a dead man could vote in Duvall County then, and they were documented as having done so there again in 1960 during the Presidential election, why can't a dead man confess to a murder in Dallas County?

And finally, why would the President of the United States personally call the operating room at Parkland Hospital and ask for a deathbed confession? That question still puzzles me. Why wouldn't someone with the Dallas police or the FBI make that request? Then, more questions followed, inquiries that had frightening, inconceivable answers.

I rushed back into the operating room and approached Dr. Shires. There was blood everywhere, and five sets of hands were working in Oswald's belly.

"You won't believe who I just talked to," I said to Dr. Shires.

He looked at me with a "what's next" expression.

"President Johnson would like for us to allow that man over there to get a statement from our patient."

Shires glanced at "Oliver Hardy," shook his head in disbelief, and returned his attention to the operation. I wish that I could have taken a picture of him as he stood there, covered in blood. It would have been worth an entire library of words in expressing our efforts to save Oswald.

Under the best circumstances, it would have been days before Oswald could have spoken lucidly to anyone. It was ironic. We had a patient on the table under oxygen anesthesia, bleeding to death from a bullet that had penetrated almost every organ in his body, and the President of the United States wanted the intruder with the gun to conduct an interview. The fact that a stranger was in the operating room during surgery, something that would have never been tolerated, best illustrates the hospital's state of confusion at that time.

Only moments later, at 12:37 P.M., almost one hour into the operation, Oswald's heart began to fail. Dr, Akin's anesthesiology resident reported to the operating team that Oswald's cardiac condition was weakening, and that his pulse rate was slowing. Electrical impulses on the cardioscope confirmed the sudden development. Dr. Shires placed his hand under Oswald's diaphragm to detect heart activity. As everyone looked on in silence, Dr. Shires shook his head and told Dr. Perry that Oswald's rhythmic cardiac activity had stopped.

I walked over to our visitor with the gun and re-marked, "There won't be any deathbed confession today." Like Clint Hill, "Oliver Hardy" disappeared, and I never saw him again. Dr. Perry grabbed a scalpel and cut open Oswald's chest by making an incision between his ribs, exposing the heart. Two injections were immediately administered directly into the heart, as additional drugs were added to the IV's. To overcome the adverse effects of the acid of anaerobic metabolism that had invaded the blood from hemorrhagic shock, we were perfusing Oswald's system with medication. Only moments later, he went into ventricular fibrillation. His heart was quivering like Jell-O.

While waiting for the voltage to build on the defibrillation machine, Dr. Perry began manual cardiac massage. To no effect, Dr. McClelland pressed the paddles to Oswald's trembling organ and administered a jolt of electric current. Again, he embraced the heart with the conductors and applied a shock, this time stronger than the previous one. The muscle jumped, but it was to no avail. In spite of escalating the voltage each time, Dr. McClelland could not restart the heartbeat. Dr. Perry again administered manual cardiac massage, but Oswald's color had turned blue because of the lack of oxygen. Dr. Shires examined his eyes. His lenses were opaque. It was 1:07 P.M., and Lee Harvey Oswald was dead.

For several moments we stood there in silence, gazing at a dead man who had possibly taken the secrets and evidence of Kennedy's assassination to the grave. Outside of President Kennedy, this was the one patient we did not want to lose. We truly believed that we had a chance to save Oswald. Had the ambulance that brought him to Parkland been furnished with equipment and emergency medical technicians to administer oxygen through an endotracheal tube and dispense Ringer's lactate through IV's, resuscitation could have occurred at the scene of the shooting.

Oswald did not die from damaged internal organs. He died from the chemical imbalances of hemorrhagic shock. From the time he was shot, 11:21 A.M., until the moment fluids were introduced into the body through cutdowns, 11:40 A.M., there was very little blood circulating in Oswald's body. As a result, he was not getting oxygen, and waste built up in his cells. Then, when the fluids were started, the collection of waste from the cells was dumped into the bloodstream, suddenly increasing the acid level, and delivering these impurities to his heart. When the contaminated blood reached the heart, it went into arrest, then cardiac arrhythmia, and finally fibrillation. The drugs that were injected directly into Oswald's heart were intended to stabilize the muscle, but the damage couldn't be reversed. His heart had stopped and couldn't be started again.

If Ringer's lactate had begun flowing into Oswald when the ambulance arrived at the police station, he would not have been without circulation for twenty minutes, the waste would not have built up in his cells, and his heart, in all probability, wouldn't have stopped. If today's emergency care had been available in 1963, Lee Harvey Oswald could have lived, because he would have been brought into the hospital in a more stable condition. All the damage caused by the bullet could have been repaired with every expectation of a full recovery.

While the bullet was removed from Oswald's right side and turned over to the legal authorities waiting outside the operating room, we began preparing to go downstairs to a conference room packed with journalists eagerly waiting to get word on Oswald's condition. I gave Dr. Shires a clean white coat. His was covered with blood.

We dreaded going into the news conference to report the death of President Kennedy's accused assassin. When we entered the room, our solemn glares told the story. Doctors are notorious for maintaining "game faces" (somberness) in the full view of adversity, but there must have been a clear message in the way we looked that afternoon. Those reporters knew Oswald was dead before a word was ever spoken.

Dr. Shires walked to the microphone. We were standing directly behind him. He announced that the accused assassin, Lee Harvey Oswald, had expired at 1:07 P.M., while in surgery. That everything humanly possible was done to save him, but that the adverse effects of hemorrhagic shock could not be overcome. Then Dr. Shires asked if there were any questions. Of all that had happened during those three days, the very first inquiry by a newsman in the first row may have topped it all. He asked, "Doc, is he dead?" From that moment on, my opinion of the press took a steep dive. Other, more intelligent questions were along the lines of wanting to know if Oswald had said anything before he had died, and why he couldn't be saved.

It's amazing to me that, during those three days, we treated hundreds of people who were wheeled into the emergency room, so mangled and torn that death should have been certain. But some way, most of them managed to live. Yet, we could not salvage the life of the President or his accused assassin.

For years, I have replayed our performance that weekend in 1963, and I keep coming to the same conclusion—neither of them could be saved. Parkland had superlative surgeons, state-of-the-art equipment, and it was an early mecca of medical research for trauma. I'm convinced beyond any doubt that President Kennedy or Lee Harvey Oswald, in the same condition that we received them at Parkland, would have died in any hospital in the world.

When Dr. Shires had concluded the meeting, I ducked out a back exit and headed for the parking lot. All the way to my car, reporters were at my heels, requesting an interview and barking questions. Ignoring all their attempts to get a story from me, I jumped into my automobile and drove home. When I arrived at my apartment, I found the place full of people—more bedlam. All my neighbors, friends, and in-laws were there, waiting to quiz me on every detail of the previous three days. And again, I carefully chose my words to tell them almost nothing, for I never knew when one of the men in suits might be just outside my window, listening.

3:00 P.M.
Washington, D.C.

Walter Jenkins, President Johnson's assistant and right-hand man, converses by phone
with FBI Director J. Edgar Hoover. Hoover
tells Jenkins, "There is nothing further on the
Oswald case except that he is dead . . . Oswald having been killed today, after our
warnings to the Dallas Police Department,
was inexcusable. It will allow, I am afraid, a
lot of civil rights people to raise a lot of hell
because he was handcuffed and had no
weapon. There are bound to be some elements of our society who will holler their
heads off that his civil rights were violated—
which they were." (Emphasis added)

FBI Headquarters—Dallas

FBI Special Agent in Charge J. Gordon
Shanklin calls Agent James Hosty into his office. Shanklin is holding the note Oswald had
delivered to the agency a couple of weeks
before the assassination. He passes it to
Hosty and says, "Here, get rid of it." Hosty,
obeying his superior, takes the note to the
toilet and flushes it away. The existence of

the note was kept secret until twelve years after the President's murder. Its contents have never been revealed. (Only two things can really be surmised about the contents of the note. One, it would *not* have helped point the finger of guilt at Oswald, and two, it *would* have caused the FBI great embarrassment.)

And it was this agency, the FBI, which was given "full responsibility" for the investigation of the murders of John Kennedy and Lee Oswald by the new President, Lyndon Baines Johnson.

Evening

Home—Dallas

I wanted to know what the networks were saying about Oswald, Parkland, and Dallas, but there were too many people in the house to turn on the television. By 10:30 P.M., everyone had left and the telephone finally stopped ringing. At last, I was sitting alone in my living room, my shoes off, and a cold beer in my hand. Earlier that day there had been advertisements for a program that was to air immediately after the late news, which would be a synopsis of the events over the past three days. I turned on the Sylvania, propped my feet, and lit a cigarette.

The program opened with a film clip of President Kennedy and Jacqueline in Fort Worth at the Hotel Texas. From there, their path was documented to Love Field in Dallas. As the scene changed to show the motorcade traveling through downtown Dallas, I began to feel anxious. When I saw the Presidential limousine approaching the Texas School Book Depository, my body stiffened.

Several minutes later the focus of the program changed to Oswald. It showed him being arrested. He told a newsman that he hadn't shot President Kennedy. Then the camera switched to two men escorting Oswald into the basement of the Dallas city jail, the narrator explaining that the accused assassin was being transferred to the county jail. Suddenly, a man in a hat lunged from the crowd of people and shot Oswald. I simply could not believe what my eyes had witnessed. I remember the grimace on Oswald's face. He had good reason to exhibit pain. I had seen what the bullet from that gun had done to his abdomen.

Treating trauma victims is bad enough without also seeing the barbaric acts inflicted upon them. Having seen all I could stand, I turned off the television and went to bed. Even after closing my eyes, I continued to see the images and events of the past three days in vivid detail against a black background—insanity in silhouette.

EPILOGUE

One summer evening in 1989, I was attending a medical meeting in downtown Dallas. When it had concluded, I began my drive back to Fort Worth. I was headed west on Elm Street, which ties into Stemmons Expressway that leads north to Parkland Hospital. Being almost midnight, there was very little traffic. As I approached the Texas School Book Depository Building at the corner of Houston and Elm, I got the same eerie feeling I always have when I pass by that location. This time I decided to park and get out of my car. Although I have driven by it hundreds of times, this was the first time that I had actually stopped and walked toward the building. Perhaps I had avoided it because of the memories that had lingered for so many years.

Even at that late hour, several people were milling around that fateful spot. Day or night, someone is always there, going through the same routine, looking up at the sixth floor from where shots were fired, then staring at the grassy knoll, from where more shots were fired.

I parked my car and began making the one-half

block pilgrimage down the descending Elm Street until I reached the exact location where the President had been shot. I got a chill that began at the back of my neck and ran down to my toes.

Imagination took over. I looked up at that sixth floor and saw a man with a rifle. Turning to the grassy knoll, I heard shots, and saw the President clutch his throat and lean slightly forward. Then more shots ring out. Connally grimaces with pain, collapsing into his wife's lap, just before the President's head explodes and recoils backward from the force of the missile. In a second, in my mind's eye, I saw the events unfold, people screaming, blood, brains, utter bedlam.

"Good evening," a young man standing beside me whispered, as if speaking at a normal volume would have been disrespectful.

Escaping the mirage of Kennedy's limousine disappearing into the triple underpass, I replied, "Hello. Do you come here often?"

"No, this is my first time. I'm from Wisconsin." He hesitated for a moment as he glanced up at the sixth floor of the Texas School Book Depository Building. "I have to leave early in the morning, and I wanted to be here just for a few minutes."

"What do you think happened?" I asked.

"Lee Harvey Oswald shot President Kennedy from up there," he replied confidently, pointing to the famous window.

"What about there?" I asked, pointing to the grassy knoll area. He shrugged in indifference.

"Where were you on November 22, 1963?" I continued.

"In a baby bed, probably," he answered, then chuckled. "Where were you?"

"Me?" I hesitated for several seconds. "I was working in a hospital, watching a man die. I'm a doctor."

"Who do you think really killed him?" he asked.

"I don't know."

The young man smiled and nodded good-bye, then turned and left. His question continued to reverberate through my mind. Who killed John F. Kennedy?

The passing of twenty-eight years has not softened the horror of those moments nor diminished the troubling images of that weekend in 1963. A thousand times a thousand, I have relived that terrible hour when I stood, helplessly watching the last drops of life seep from the President's body. Then, two days later, we tried to save Lee Harvey Oswald after he had essentially bled to death before being rolled into the emergency room.

More disturbing than the images of President Kennedy are the questions about President Johnson. Why did he insist that Kennedy's body be placed on board *Air Force One* before returning to Washington? Why did he personally call Captain Will Fritz of the Dallas Homicide Department, telling him that he had his man, and that no further investigation was needed? Why did he personally call me at Parkland about a confession from Oswald? Why would a President with the immediate and monumental task of taking over the U.S. government involve himself in a matter that should have been routinely handled by the law enforcement agencies? Why did he usurp the authority of the Texas officials and place the responsibility for the investigation in the hands of a personal crony, FBI head J. Edgar Hoover? No doubt, the operations of murder and cover-up required no less than a sovereign figure who, first, had the influence, power, and knowledge to carry out the deed. Second, and more difficult, such a person must cover up the act through the manipulation of information. Only one man had such power on November 22, 1963, and he became President of the United States. Paramount to this operation of obscurity was the appointment of the Warren Commission and the locking up of vital information for seventy-five years—both of which were the acts of Lyndon Baines Johnson.

And above all, what was meant by Johnson's curious and perhaps prophetic pronouncement, seven months before the trip to Texas, when he said ". . . the President of the United States is like a pilot and the election is when the Nation picks an airplane and a pilot for the next four years. Once you pick him, and you're flying across the water in bad weather don't go up and open the door and try to knock him in the head. He's the only pilot you have, and if the plane goes down, you go with it. *At least wait until next November before you shoot him down.*" (Emphasis added) November 1963 was not a Presidential election year, and Johnson, an extremely clever politician, knew it.

Parkland Hospital was placed in the untenable position of bringing back to life two important men who had been afforded the most inept and incompetent protection ever provided. In the President's case, the Secret Service agents assigned to him had gotten drunk the evening before he was shot. As for Oswald, the Dallas police allowed a virtual gangster to stand within only a few feet of the man accused of assassinating the President of the United States.

We did all we could do for those two men. We did all anyone could do, but the dead cannot be brought to life again. President Kennedy was neurologically dead when he was wheeled into Parkland. In the case of Oswald, had a modern-day emergency medical system been available, he could probably have lived. Now, ambulances fully furnished with state-of-the-art resuscitation equipment are dispatched to the victim within three minutes, the most critical time period for a trauma injury. Thanks to skilled paramedics and medical technicians, the patient receives the same treatment at the accident scene that he would at Parkland Hospital. Ringer's lactate applied through IV's, electrocardiograms, shocks to the heart, and constant communication with a physician in the hospital's emergency room enable medical personnel to provide life-saving care that could have made the difference in Oswald.

More frustrating than the assassination itself was the behavior of government officials and the people who blamed Parkland for both deaths. These, as well as the deceit of the Warren Report, are the reasons I decided to research and then write this book. Had I not been in those emergency rooms and experienced the subsequent intimidation and criticism, I would have never made the commitment to tell the story.

That the real story has not been told is a tragedy. The thought of a conspiracy to kill the President, plus the power to obscure it through the Warren Commission, led me to the obvious conclusion—people within our government, in concert with the "silverfish" of our society, murdered the President of the United States. It was a coup d'etat—no better than a thirty-second revolution in a third-rate country, a thousand of which have been seen on movie screens, which bring thoughts of "never in America."

In the case of the physicians and medical personnel at Parkland Hospital, the conspiracy of silence was a mixture of fraternal doctrine, naïveté, fear, and career-mindedness. This career-mindedness can best be summarized in Dr. Charles Baxter's decree: "We made an opening statement to everybody concerned that if anybody on the medical side ever made a dime off the assassination, we'd see to it that they never went anywhere in medicine again because that's how strongly we felt that this was a private thing."

The true conspiracy of silence and the fraternal doctrine that gives it life is found more explicitly in the action and inaction of other groups and individuals connected in some way to the President's death. Included in, but not limited to, this association are the President's family and aides, the new President and his aides, government employees, military officials, the FBI, the Secret Service, the CIA, Texas law enforcement personnel, local and national news media, Dealey Plaza witnesses, Jack Ruby's and Lee Harvey Oswald's friends and acquaintances, as well as the military pathology team and its witnesses.

Think of this collection of people, organizations, and events as a mass of spaghetti, each strand representing someone or something related to John F. Kennedy's death. So entangled and convoluted are they that it is almost impossible to trace any one element or person to a conclusion. There is no beginning or ending—no clear path progressing to a final resolution—just more leads twisted around dead ends that disappear into a pile of confusion.

Many of the people in these groups knew they were telling lies that were accepted as facts; they knew that their silence was ordered; they knew that the evidence was fabricated, falsified, and destroyed; and they knew that witnesses were intimidated, ignored, and inadequately interrogated.

Recently, on the "Phil Donahue Show," Richard Helms, former CIA director, provided viewers with a rare and revealing glimpse into the reality of this phenomenon when he answered the question, why don't people speak up? "People don't speak up," Helms said, "at the time for several reasons. One, they don't know the facts at the time. Secondly, in all of these cover-ups—for example the Secret Service knew all about John Kennedy's womanizing—but they had a CONSPIRACY OF SILENCE. Why? Because they worked for John F. Kennedy! It is very difficult in real time to get people to talk, particularly when there may be sanctions against them—and the young lady who is twenty-five, who wants to take on one of these powerful figures sometime by saying something she knows about them, does so at her own peril. Ahhh, I don't want to emphasize that anything is going to be done to her, *but by the time the newspapers, or somebody, gets through with her she'll wish she hadn't done it.*" (Emphasis added)

From the silence of the people involved came a great miscarriage of justice and an almost complete loss of faith by the American people in their government and its agencies. Due to their active or passive participation in the continuing cover-up, we are faced, twenty-eight years after the fact, with the still unsolved murder of one of the world's greatest leaders. The assassination was a brutal action that changed our domestic and foreign policy, and reshaped history. The individuals involved in this conspiracy of silence are neither heroes nor great Americans. At best, they may be considered cowards . . . at worst, coconspirators or accessories after the fact. This conspiracy must end.

PART 3:
UPDATES 2013

1

REFLECTIONS

Jens Hansen

Dr. Charles A. Crenshaw spent the final ten years of his life in steadfast defense of a truth that he tenaciously and tirelessly claimed exposed a very big lie about medical evidence and the Warren Commission Report (WCR). Dr. Crenshaw died on November 15, 2001.

The lie, Dr. Crenshaw firmly asserted, was the Warren Commission's claim that all the bullets that struck President John F. Kennedy and Governor John Connally were fired by the sole gunman, Lee Harvey Oswald, from the sixth floor of the Texas School Book Depository in Dealey Plaza. This firing position above and behind the limousine, according to Dr. Crenshaw and other Parkland Memorial Hospital doctors, was incompatible with President Kennedy's fatal gunshot wounds.

According to Dr. Crenshaw and other experts, the truth is the bullets that struck President Kennedy in his head and throat were fired from position(s) facing the President's limousine by one or more gunmen, who were never identified or brought to justice. This firing position is consistent with at least two of President Kennedy's wounds, including the shot that killed him.

One or more shots fired from in front of and toward the limousine meant there were at least two gunmen. This is why Dr. Crenshaw's assessment of the president's wounds was, and still is, untenable to the individuals, government agencies and forces still defending the Warren Commission Report.

Gunshots from the infamous grassy knoll area, which was located in front of the president's limousine, were heard by people standing in Dealey Plaza the moment President Kennedy was shot. When the shots rang out, the president grasped with both hands toward his throat where the bullet had struck him. Seconds later, another bullet entered his forehead and blew his brains and scalp backward onto the trunk of the limousine.

Since 1963, that has been the entire essence of the conspiracy war that has raged in millions of words, printed on thousands and thousands of pages, bound in libraries of books. Dr. Crenshaw believed that the uncorrupted medical evidence definitively answered that critical question. Once that question was answered, even after fifty years, all other issues become moot because the assassination of President Kennedy will forever remain a cold case file.

Dr. Crenshaw was never interested in

assassination conspiracy theories. He was never on a mission to discover who shot President Kennedy. He only wanted an untainted medical record to reflect correctly that President Kennedy sustained fatal entry wounds from bullets fired from in front of his limousine. It was obvious to Dr. Crenshaw that the people now attacking him, perhaps even the two FBI agents who showed up at his front door and his office, were still protecting the Warren Commission findings.

When *JFK: Conspiracy of Silence* was published in 1992, the guardians of the twenty-eight-year Warren Commission lie came forth in a raging attack on Dr. Crenshaw. From all directions came exigent and frantic efforts to discredit him as a doctor and to minimize, even deny, his participation in performing a surgical procedure on President Kennedy and his eyewitness observations that had accurately assessed the president's mortal wounds.

During those early years as a physician, Dr. Crenshaw spent substantial time working in a big-city emergency room treating victims of the growing gun violence. He had observed battlefield wounds in war veterans when he worked as an intern at the Veterans Administration Hospital. By the time he was in his third-year surgical residency at Parkland Hospital, he had treated hundreds of urban-war gunshot victims. Moreover, as a hunter for many years, Dr. Crenshaw was familiar with how bullets from high-powered rifles damage tissue and bone. Dr. Crenshaw knew as much or more about gunshot wounds as did any other doctor in Trauma Room 1.

Dr. Crenshaw was not another self-appointed expert creating a new wrinkle in the conspiracy theory to sell books. He was one of the hands-on surgeons treating President Kennedy during the entire twenty-minute, attempted lifesaving effort. When Dr. Crenshaw personally placed the president's body in the traveling casket, he was the last surgeon at Parkland to make a close and final inspection of the wounds. So, when Dr. Crenshaw first saw the official autopsy photographs in 1991, he claimed with legitimate authority that the president's body had been fraudulently altered, which was what the Warren Commission used to justify the "single bullet" theory. That was the only reason Dr. Crenshaw wrote and published *JFK: Conspiracy of Silence.*

Dr. Crenshaw also saw three small wounds on the right side of the president's face, but the horrendous brain damage, by comparison, caused these minor injuries to be ignored. When President Kennedy was embalmed, Thomas Evan Robinson, the mortician, confirmed a small wound in the temple and two other small wounds in the face. It is believed by some researchers that one of the bullets shot at the president struck the ground in front or to the side of the limousine, causing chipped cement fragments to act as shrapnel and hit the right side of President Kennedy's face. These wounds were packed with wax.

Some researchers have suggested that when the president abruptly stopped waving, as evidenced in the Zapruder film, it was because he had heard the initial rifle shot, which missed the presidential limousine and hit the pavement on Elm Street. Of course, if the president did hear the initial gunshot, he did not have time to take evasive action to avoid being struck by the life-ending bullets that followed almost immediately thereafter.

In 1992, Thomas Evan Robinson also confirmed in an interview that during the embalming process he observed a large gaping hole in back of President Kennedy's head that had been patched with a piece of rubber. Robinson added that the president's skull appeared to have been filled with plaster of paris. Robinson also noted the smaller, three-inch, flapped-down piece of scalp in a crescent shape above the right temple area. This wound evidences the shot to the president's head, from which most people turn away when watching the Zapruder film.

Dr. Crenshaw didn't need either the revenue or the aggravation from writing such a controversial book on the assassination, nor did he savor the thought of taking on the power structure of Parkland Hospital. His only interest was in establishing the one fact that alone would be sufficient to deem the Warren Report a flawed document. If Dr. Crenshaw had not been truthful about the medical evidence he observed, the other Parkland Hospital doctors would have come out en masse with their collective notes and memory to expose him accordingly. They had observed the same medical evidence. Yet, no such effort to discredit Dr. Crenshaw was made by his fellow doctors because most of them agreed with him.

It was only because Dr. Crenshaw had retired—and his medical career was no longer at risk—that he considered coming forth with a work exposing the fraudulent autopsy photographs that proved President Kennedy's wounds were altered. Other Parkland doctors had made comments questioning the medical evidence that was delivered to Dr. James Humes for the autopsy, but no Parkland doctor prior to Dr. Crenshaw's book had published a work forensically disputing the autopsy photographs and the Warren Commission Report.

Dr. Crenshaw had waited almost twenty-nine years after the assassination to challenge the autopsy photos and the Warren Report. This decision was primarily based on Dr. Charles Baxter's promise to ruin the career of any doctor who published and profited on information or opinions about the medical evidence. Dr. Baxter would not have hesitated slightly in ruining Dr. Crenshaw's career over *JFK: Conspiracy of Silence*. This threat had stayed fresh in Dr. Crenshaw's mind. Throughout his career, he felt the presence of that threat as a canopy of secrecy and a forced "conspiracy of silence" that no doctor dared violate with a major publication.

Dr. Baxter repeated this threat in a book produced by the Community Relations Department at Parkland Memorial Hospital titled *A Sense of Mission*, covering the years 1894 through 1989. In that book, an article titled "JFK Memories Reinforce PMH Goals" contains the spoken words of Dr. Charles Baxter, who was the physician in charge of Trauma Room 1. Dr. Baxter stated: *"We made an open statement to everybody concerned that if anybody on the medical side ever made a dime off the assassination, we'd see to it that they never went anywhere in medicine ever again, because that's how strongly we felt that this was a private thing."*

By quantifying the amount of time and personal resources invested by Dr. Crenshaw, in addition to the abuse endured to correct the medical record and expose the Warren Commission lies, he did not make even a dime.

The alteration of President Kennedy's wounds and forensic evidence outraged Dr. Crenshaw and other Parkland doctors.

Accordingly, they made isolated comments from time to time that would not violate the Baxter dictum. However, Dr. Crenshaw's book about the detailed medical evidence obliterated Baxter's line in the sand. Because the other doctors were still practicing medicine in 1992, they could only privately support Dr. Crenshaw's book to expose the medical truth, even after twenty-nine years of silence. And many of them did indeed support Dr. Crenshaw. Dr. Crenshaw found to his satisfaction that he was speaking for many of the Parkland doctors. Dr. Robert Jones, professor of internal medicine of University of Texas Southwestern Medical Center at Dallas, and Dr. Robert McClelland, professor emeritus of surgery, also of UT Southwestern Medical Center, openly supported Dr. Crenshaw's book in spite of Dr. Baxter's warning.

It is important to note that Dr. Baxter did not dispute Dr. Crenshaw's claims about President Kennedy's wounds. To do so would have been dishonest, and it could have been embarrassing to Dr. Baxter. Although perhaps misguided in his self-appointed role as the don of the medical evidence, Dr. Baxter did not have a reputation for dishonesty. He is now deceased, so history will never know his real reasons for bullying the other doctors to control the information. Perhaps the government used Dr. Baxter to help contain or mold the medical evidence because the details of Dr. Baxter's testimony before the Warren Commission seemed to tell a very troubling story.

Dr. Baxter's holographic report on President Kennedy's wounds dated November 22, 1963, recorded as Exhibit 392 in Volume XVII of the *Investigation of the Assassination of President John F. Kennedy*, reads in part: *The President had a wound in the midline of the neck. On first observation of the remaining wounds, the **temporal** and **occipital** bones were missing and the brain was lying on the table with extensive lacerations and contusions.*

Credit: Clark Creber

This reading from Dr. Baxter's 1963 report is referring to the bullet wound to the president's throat and separate bullet wounds to the president's head. As to the bullet that caused the wounds to the president's head, Dr. Baxter's description indicates the injury to the occipital region of the president's skull was an exit wound. That bullet would have entered the president's temporal area and exited his occipital area. The bullet blew a large hole in the back of President Kennedy's head, which Dr. Baxter purposely, accurately and deliberately described as the occipital region of the president's skull. The force of that bullet discharged his brains, scalp and skull bones onto the trunk of the limousine and onto Elm Street. However, Dr. Baxter's wound description to the occipital was utterly and completely incompatible with the wounds Oswald would have caused by shooting the president from the sixth floor of the Texas School Book Depository building. Only shooting the president point blank from the limousine's left bumper could have physically caused a wound to the president's head as described by the government's selected pathologist, Dr James Humes.

Therefore, the Warren Commission had to exclude, expunge from its records and findings, all evidence that indicated or suggested there was an exit wound to the occipital region of the president's skull. The lead doctor in Trauma

Room 1 at Parkland Hospital was derailing the Oswald sole assassin story with his handwritten words. That meant Dr. Baxter's 1963 report had to be altered to coincide with President Kennedy's fraudulent autopsy report that showed the severe injury to the back of President Kennedy's head as an "entry" wound.

Whatever pressure, price, threat or deed needed to exact a change in Dr. Baxter's report was obviously brought to bear because on March 24, 1964, when Arlen Specter asked Dr. Baxter to read his November 22, 1963, handwritten report into the Warren Commission record, Dr. Baxter spoke the following: "The president had a wound in the midline of the neck. On first observation of the remaining wounds, the temporal and parietal bones were missing and the brain was lying on the table with extensive lacerations and contusions." Dr. Baxter had omitted the "occipital" region of President Kennedy's skull and changed it to the "parietal." In so doing, Arlen Specter apparently thought he had made the assassination scenario slightly more tenable (yet it was still laughably absurd) that Oswald alone caused all the forensic damage to President Kennedy's head with one shot from the sixth floor of the Texas School Book Depository building. The one-word change to Dr. Baxter's surgical report became the springboard for the Warren Commission to launch volumes of false information, corrupted medical evidence and incorrect conclusions.

This recitation of Dr. Baxter's 1963 hand-written notes was recorded in Volume VI of the *Investigation of the Assassination of President John F. Kennedy*.

The effect of this altered testimony meant the Warren Commission could claim, without conflicting with Dr. Baxter's report, that the bullet shot from the sixth floor of the Texas School Book Depository entered President Kennedy's head in the parietal region of his skull and exited his temporal region. This one-word change to Dr. Baxter's initial 1963 report altered it from an "exit" wound to an "entry" wound. That's how desperate Arlen Specter was to conform all evidence and testimony—by using whatever method necessary—to support the Oswald sole assassin story.

Undoubtedly, the Warren Commission and Arlen Specter believed they had dodged the proverbial bullet by changing Dr. Baxter's testimony. Tampering with evidence is a crime, a felony, especially in a Texas homicide case. The average citizen would go to prison for a long time for altering evidence in a capital murder case.

Indisputably, the Warren Commission had conformed Dr. Baxter's report to fit Humes's gerrymandered autopsy report whereby a bullet entered the parietal region and exited the temporal region of the president's skull. This, of course, places a whole new meaning behind the dire warning Dr. Baxter issued the doctors in Trauma Room 1.

Because Dr. Crenshaw published *JFK: Conspiracy of Silence,* Dr. Baxter terminated their lifelong friendship as retribution. Dr. Baxter was obviously sensitive to anyone who would divulge information that would draw attention to his changed testimony. The punitive measure taken against Dr. Crenshaw proved Charlie Baxter's threat to those doctors had always remained in force and in effect—no matter who violated it. Dr. Baxter had crowned himself "King of Trauma Room 1" and was not reluctant to punish anyone violating his decree.

Privately, one of Dr. Crenshaw's greatest fears was that the same people and forces that assassinated the president and threatened Dr. Earl Rose might also murder him for publishing his book. He knew there would be substantial fallout. From the moment *JFK: Conspiracy of Silence* went public, Dr. Crenshaw's life became chaotic. It was like he and his wife, Susan, had walked through a door into a new and unexpected world. Dr. Crenshaw's story was being watched all across America and around the globe. It was big news, bigger than Dr. Crenshaw had ever anticipated.

The book zoomed to number one on the *New York Times* Best Sellers list on April 26, 1992, and stayed there for thirteen weeks.

There were forty-plus messages a day on his home telephone. He had immediately come under vicious verbal attacks with some death threats. Dr. Crenshaw posed a real problem for those people still protecting the Warren Commission Report. Dr. Crenshaw had, in essence, exhumed President Kennedy's body and was showing the world the unaltered wounds.

Who were the people attacking Dr. Crenshaw for disputing the autopsy photographs and the 1964 Warren Report? Some attacks came from irrelevant Kennedy buffs turned detectives who had asserted themselves into the assassination. Many of these people were jealous attention seekers who were miles from Trauma Room 1 and not relevant at all to the assassination. Such self-appointed experts continue to make noise from the periphery while criticizing and doubting highly trained eyewitnesses, like Dr. Crenshaw. Regarding these Kennedy tailgaters, Dr. Crenshaw said that John McAdams was one of the most vocal, ignorant and obnoxious, and he "would not know a bullet wound from a doughnut hole."

Along with the attacks, Dr. Crenshaw also received wide support for his book throughout America and the world. For example, by special invitation, he and his wife traveled to 1 Wimpole Street in downtown London, headquarters of The Royal Society of Medicine. There they lodged as the Royal Society's guests and were warmly received when Dr. Crenshaw delivered a medical lecture on the true wounds of President Kennedy and how they had been altered. Dr. Crenshaw found that the English people took great interest in the assassination of President Kennedy and believed the Warren Commission Report to be a real "corker." Additionally, Dr. Crenshaw was invited to give lectures throughout England and Scotland. Besides the English-language version, the book was printed in Japanese, French and German.

In November 1963, the physicians at Parkland Memorial Hospital had unfortunately spent critical time trying to bring President Kennedy back from the dead. Doctors bring patients back from the dead every day. Electric paddles restart recalcitrant hearts fallen silent. Even the faintest hint of a heartbeat was enough to invoke the Parkland doctors into extreme lifesaving measures, notwithstanding the fact the president could not have survived with the brain trauma he suffered.

There were two open portals in the president's skull from which critical brain matter had been blown out. Consider the irony and the visual scene of highly trained physicians and surgeons deploying plenary lifesaving procedures on a man whose brains had been strewn from Dealey Plaza to Parkland Memorial

Hospital. Remaining brain tissue dangled
tenuously from his scalp and hair. That composite mental picture best illustrates the insanity that day.

In those first moments of horror in Dealey
Plaza, Jacqueline Kennedy instinctively crawled
out onto the trunk of their limousine to retreat
and retrieve her husband's brains and scalp. All
the doctors in the emergency room had acted
with the same instincts as Jacqueline in their
limousine. But the doctors in Trauma Room 1
had to know the president was dead from the
moment he was rolled into the hospital. Dr.
Crenshaw said as much. Kennedy's eyes were
"fixed and void of life."

Jacqueline Kennedy later recalled that she
could see a flesh-colored piece of her husband's
skull detach from his head. She realized she was
holding his hair over a gaping hole in the back
of President Kennedy's skull. Jacqueline said
when she saw the hole, she knew then that
her husband was dead. This was the occipital
wound. The Warren Commission omitted this
information about the president's wounds from
the official report because such a large hole
would be where the bullet exited his head.
That omission was not discovered until several
years later. It is not surprising that the Warren
Commission avoided all evidence from multiple witnesses and sources of a gaping hole in
the back of President Kennedy's head. Such a

bullet wound did not bode well for the feigned story of a bullet entering the back of the president's head *instead of exiting* the back of the president's head. A gaping hole in the back of President Kennedy's skull did not support sole assassin Oswald shooting from behind the limousine. An exit wound in the back of the president's skull meant someone shot him from in front of the limousine.

Five decades of reflection on the Kennedy assassination harden some facts. "I think I may have a pulse. He may have a heartbeat" were mere declarations of hopeful caregivers rather than announcements of reality in Trauma Room 1. According to the publication *A Sense of Mission:* "There was no pulse, no real blood pressure. Only an infrequent heartbeat," Dr. Baxter said when President Kennedy was logged into the register at 12:38 P.M. as patient No. 24740.

Rolled into a hospital with the same fatal wounds, the average citizen would not be a candidate for any of the lifesaving procedures given President Kennedy. They would be summarily sent to the medical examiner's office for an autopsy.

Dr. Crenshaw and other doctors in the room believed Kennedy was immutably dying the second the bullet ripped through the president's head. Yet, there was implicit agreement among the doctors that lifesaving measures had to be expended liberally to give a dead man the chance to rise. That decision and the time it wasted would result in a monumental tragedy unto itself.

"My God, the whole right side of his head is shot off . . . . We've nothing to work with," Dr. Kemp Clark exclaimed when he entered the room and looked at the condition of the president's head. There was not even a slight hesitation in Dr. Clark declaring that the life of President Kennedy was at an end. Unfortunately, Dr. Clark, Parkland's neurosurgeon, did not examine President Kennedy until almost twenty minutes had elapsed from the time other doctors began treating him.

If Dr. Clark had pronounced the president dead when Kennedy had first been wheeled into the hospital, Dr. Rose, the pathologist, could have invested those twenty minutes in an autopsy. The autopsy evidence would have come from analyzing uncorrupted and unaltered wounds, which had not yet been sabotaged to bolster the Oswald story. According to Texas law, the forensic truth of the assassination had to be told by Dr. Rose and sent to the courts for trial. That was the significance of the Parkland doctors wasting critical time trying to revive a dead man.

Yet, the doctors trying to save President Kennedy were unaware that the federal government—led by Secret Service agent Roy

Kellerman, with automatic weapons locked and loaded—would soon usher President Kennedy's body out of the hospital and into a colossal controversy. A quick death pronouncement and immediate autopsy would have saved the country from the enormous Warren Commission lie and spared the country decades of the controversy surrounding it. There had been only minutes to establish truthful and legitimate forensic evidence and a chain of custody beginning with Dr. Rose. The federal government completely ignored two Texas statutes when President Kennedy's body was forcefully taken from Parkland Hospital and flown to Maryland without an autopsy.

First Statute: Section 1. Article 968, Code of Criminal Procedure of the State of Texas, 1925, be, and is hereby amended to read as follows: "Any Justice of the Peace shall be authorized, and it shall be his duty, to hold inquests without a jury within the County in the following cases . . . 2. When any person is killed; or from any cause dies an unnatural death. . . ."
Section 3, That Article 970: "An inquest held to ascertain the cause of death, the Justice of the Peace shall in all cases call in the county health officer, or if there be none, or if his services are not then obtainable, then a duly licensed and practicing physician, shall procure their opinions and advice as to the necessity of an autopsy before reaching determinations as to whether or not to order an autopsy

to determine the cause of death. . . ." Approved and effective June 12, 1947

<u>Second Statute</u>: *"An Act providing proper parties to give consent on bodies of deceased persons: Acts 1953., 53rd Legislature., p. 573. ch. 216." Effective May 27, 1953*

OFFICE AUTHORIZED
Section 1. Subject to the provisions of this Act, the Commissioners Court of any county having a population of more than five hundred thousand (500,000) . . . shall establish and maintain the office of Medical Examiner.

DEATH INVESTIGATIONS
Section 6. Any Medical Examiner, or his duly authorized deputy, shall be authorized, and it shall be his duty, to hold inquests with or without a jury within his county, in the following cases:

1. *When a person shall die within 24 hours after admission to a hospital or institution or in prison or in jail.*
2. *When any person is killed; or from any cause dies an unnatural death. . . .*
4. *When the circumstances of the death of any person are such as to lead to suspicion that he came to his death by unlawful means.*

AUTOPSY
Section 9. If the cause of death shall be determined beyond a reasonable doubt as a result of the investigation, the Medical Examiner shall file a report thereof setting forth specifically the cause of death with the District Attorney or Criminal District Attorney. . . . If in the opinion of the

*Medical Examiner an autopsy is necessary . . .
the autopsy will be immediately performed by
the Medical Examiner. . . .*

PENALTY
*Section 13. Any person in violation of any provi-
sion of this Act, upon conviction, shall be punished
by a fine of not more than Five Hundred Dollars
($500) or by imprisonment in the county jail for
not more than thirty (30) days, or both such fine
and imprisonment. . . .*

Dr. Rose was justified in attempting to block
Roy Kellerman from taking President Kennedy's body to protect it from tampering to
guarantee that the killers would be convicted
in a Texas court of law. The assassination of
President Kennedy in November 1963 did not
violate a federal statute. The Texas court was
the only available jurisdiction to prosecute
those who may have played a role in the assassination.

The chain of custody was breached and the
evidence was forever tainted when Kellerman
and his men forcibly removed President Kennedy's body from Parkland Hospital. As a
result, if Lee Harvey Oswald had not been
murdered, the medical evidence from Parkland
Hospital would not have been admissible in a
Texas criminal court to try him for crimes.

Documenting the wounds at Parkland Hospital as evidence of a homicide would have established the first link in the chain of custody

that would have been sent on to the Dallas County District Attorney and to the Texas court for a trial. Moreover, the death scene was never properly secured for investigation. In fact, it was thoroughly contaminated by panicking people and law enforcement authorities, who, in utter chaos, had trampled throughout Dealey Plaza after President Kennedy was assassinated.

Due to the altered medical evidence, the American people got an autopsy with no validity or legitimacy. As it were, the medical evidence was seized by bad actors to mold and to shape and to fit the Oswald story, which benefited the other shooters and the forces behind them. For Dr. Rose's attempt to follow Texas laws to conduct an autopsy on the president's body and establish the first vital link in the chain of custody, he was almost gunned down in Parkland Hospital.

Dr. Earl Rose's concerns were borne out when the president's body was flown to Bethesda, Maryland, and delivered to Dr. James Humes, the doctor who hadn't conducted an autopsy in over twenty years and had never conducted an autopsy on a gunshot victim. Dr. Humes had become the chief of anatomic pathology at the Bethesda Naval Hospital in 1960. A year later, he was made director of the laboratories at the National Medical Center. It was at this time that he was given the assignment to conduct the autopsy on President Kennedy. The autopsy was so farcically conducted that Dr. Humes didn't realize until told by Dr. Malcolm Perry at Parkland that there was a bullet entry wound to the president's throat.

Why did the government select a pathologist whose career in pathology had been in mothballs for two decades to conduct the most important autopsy in American history? There is only one plausible answer: The government wanted the autopsy to tell a story that all the bullets that struck President Kennedy were shot by Oswald, the single assassin, from behind the presidential limousine. What better pathologist to assign this task to than Dr. Humes, an old team player who would take orders like a good medical soldier? His naval career obviously had taught him the military tenet that profit for prudence was greatly preferred to punishment for principle.

Dr. James J. Humes certified that he burned certain preliminary draft notes relating to Naval Medical School Autopsy Report A63-272. He handed all other papers related to the autopsy, including the holograph draft of the final report and his notes stained with the president's blood, to his superior, Commanding Officer J. H. Stover Jr. Concerned that bloodstained notes could fall into the hands of people who would capitalize on its commercial value, Dr. Humes told the Warren Commission that he retained not even copies of his notes and report.

Dr. Pierre Finck and J. Thornton Boswell assisted Dr. Humes in the president's autopsy. A 1996 interview revealed that Dr. Humes's testimony differed from the other two doctors regarding the examination of President Kennedy's brain. During his testimony before the Assassination Records Review Board, Dr. Humes did not mention that Dr. Finck was even present at the examination, and Dr. Finck testified that the brain examination occurred much later than the time to which Dr. Humes testified. With such variations in their testimony, it became apparent there were at least two examinations of the president's brain.

James Humes Jr., son of Dr. Humes, was credited with saying his father did not want people to profit from the tragedy of an American president's death by sensationalism, like the writing of books to advance conspiracy theories. That is almost verbatim the sentiments and concerns of Dr. Baxter in Trauma Room 1 at Parkland Hospital, and apparently for the same reason. How else could they have justified altering and destroying evidence that proved drastic changes in the president's head wounds had occurred after leaving Parkland Hospital in Dallas to arriving at Bethesda Hospital in Maryland?

At every level and every stop, the same excuse was being exercised to avoid transparency and prevent the dissemination of critical and truthful medical evidence to expose the guilty parties behind the assassination. The government was intent at holding the Oswald battle line and was not to be outflanked by uncorrupted medical evidence.

Between the concerns of Dr. Baxter at Parkland Memorial Hospital and Dr. Humes at Bethesda Naval Hospital that someone might market the president's medical evidence, the historical record on the assassination suffered terribly and possibly allowed responsible parties to go unnamed and unprosecuted.

Every doctor and nurse at Parkland Hospital involved with treating President Kennedy had seen a bullet entry wound in the front of his throat and two head wounds, including a large exit hole in the back of his skull. Yet neither of these wounds is noted to be present in appearance or description in Dr. Humes's autopsy. The neck entry wound was partially obscured by the tracheostomy performed at Parkland, but the wound area had been drastically enlarged by the time it arrived at Bethesda. The hole in the back of his head had been patched after the president's body left Parkland Hospital.

The president's autopsy was beyond the independent control of Dr. Humes. He testified about that to the Warren Commission, saying his autopsy was compromised because he had limited access—to no access at all—to important X-rays and photographs. His poor autopsy report demanded some kind of explanation or excuse. Only a "company man" would certify to its accuracy by signing the report. That is why a retired naval pathologist with a pension was selected to perform the autopsy—to play ball, to do his duty by ignoring the evidence and looking the other way—then say the shoddy work wasn't his fault.

As an example, a piece of the president's occipital bone blown from the back of his head was discovered on Elm Street in Dealey Plaza. It was being analyzed and photographed in Dallas at approximately the same time the ostensible same piece of anatomy was being seen in the X-rays of President Kennedy's skull at Bethesda Hospital. In other words, a piece of the president's skull being photographed at Bethesda was a fake. Would we suppose Dr. Humes did not know, and therefore did not make note, that some substance to fake a piece of bone had been added to the president's skull to substitute for the actual piece of the president's cranium that was simultaneously being examined in Dallas? In Dr. Humes's defense, if it had not been he who was selected to conduct a corrupted autopsy, it would have been another military doctor who would have followed the same orders.

As a third-year resident surgeon, Dr. Crenshaw was not requested to submit notes to the Warren Commission for his participation in surgically treating President Kennedy. This fortuitously allowed him to declare in 1992, without any contradiction or equivocation, that the autopsy photographs proved President Kennedy's wounds examined in Maryland were not the same wounds that he saw at Parkland Hospital in 1963. The autopsy photographs Dr. Crenshaw had seen in 1991 were the basis of his claim that the Warren Report was a fundamental lie.

Fifteen medical personnel present in Trauma Room 1 were called to testify before the Warren Commission. However, four physicians present in Trauma Room One1 were not asked for testimony: Dr. Charles Crenshaw, Dr. Robert Grossman, Dr. Donald Seldin and Dr. William Zedelitz. There was speculation that, if deposed, their testimony would not have supported the single-bullet theory, which would have disagreed with the highly protected and scripted official record being established. It cannot be speculated how those doctors would have testified about the single-bullet theory, but it is safe to conclude they would have felt no less compelled to protect their medical careers than the other doctors from Dr. Baxter's demand for silence.

Where was the gaping wound where a bullet had torn a hole in the back of President

Kennedy's skull? The outline of a flap of scalp and bone in the back of President Kennedy's head are partially seen in one of the color autopsy photographs. Dr. Paul Peters had testified before the Warren Commission that he observed such a wound in the cerebellum area of the president's head, which is just below the occipital area. In 1988, Dr. McClelland said, "Somebody is concealing the whole plot. There was somebody on the grassy knoll who shot at the president and blew his head off."

Why would the U.S. Department of Justice (DOJ) come to Parkland Hospital and sabotage the medical evidence that would have been critical to prosecute Lee Harvey Oswald or other parties involved in assassinating the president? Robert Kennedy was the attorney general, the top prosecutor in the United States. He surely knew the importance of protecting evidence in a case to prosecute the individuals who murdered the president of the United States. He also knew the jurisdiction for that trial would be Texas. In 1963, assassinating President Kennedy was not a federal crime. One has to wonder, then, why was it not of paramount importance to Robert Kennedy to secure and protect the forensic evidence to convict his brother's murderers?

Perhaps the shock of losing a brother to such a horrific crime prevented Robert Kennedy from considering these important legal issues. However, someone associated with the DOJ gave the order to return President Kennedy's body, without any regard for Texas laws for prosecuting the culprits.

Oswald was arrested about the same time the president's body was forcibly removed from Parkland Hospital. Oswald would not be murdered for almost another forty-eight hours. Therefore, preserving the medical evidence at Parkland was still crucial to Texas capital murder charges, which would have been filed against Oswald. Yet, the most important evidence to that case was being intentionally tainted beyond redemption and use. Had Oswald lived, his defense attorney would have surely challenged admitting any medical evidence, including any results from James J. Humes's autopsy. Texas law had been broken when President Kennedy's body was prematurely removed from Parkland Hospital. Whoever ordered the men with guns to stop the Parkland doctors from establishing a chain of custody for the forensic evidence was either afraid of the truth or knew the medical evidence would not be needed to try a dead suspect.

The story of the infamous gurney at Parkland Memorial Hospital, where the "magic bullet" was discovered, is no less alarming. The gurney where—ostensibly—Governor John

Connally had lain and been unattended for forty-five minutes, along with a second and identical gurney, had been left next to a hospital restroom in a first-floor corridor. During that forty-five-minute period, the gurneys were moved by hospital personnel. According to hospital attendant Darrell Tomlinson, when he returned, the two gurneys were not in their same positions and a bullet rolled out from under the mat on the gurney Tomlinson believed might have possibly been Connally's. A bullet matching Oswald's rifle easily could have been planted under the gurney's mat during the forty-five minutes it was unattended. These facts committed the "magic bullet" to a death sentence as credible, potential evidence to convict a murderer in a Texas courtroom.

Under the rules of evidence, a piece of physical evidence is not admissible in a trial unless the chain of custody can be proven from beginning to end. With regard to the "magic bullet," questions abound as to whether a judge hearing a criminal case involving the president's assassination would find that the "magic bullet" was indeed connected to the case. With the lengthy gap in time between Governor Connally being moved from the gurney for surgery and the "magic bullet" appearing on one of the gurneys, it is a compelling legal question as to whether the two are, in fact, connected.

Therefore, would a judge bound by the rules

of evidence allow such a bullet to convict Oswald of shooting Connally, if Oswald had even shot a rifle? That bullet had not yet been connected to assassinating the president. Absent evidence directly or circumstantially connecting Oswald to the actual shooting of President Kennedy, a prosecution of Oswald would have to be based on his actions as an accomplice or co-conspirator acting with the assistance of another gunman or gunmen. Although the Warren Commission was not bound by the same rules of evidence that would govern a criminal trial arising out of the assassination of President Kennedy, it should have risen to an even higher standard of care to answer one of the most important questions of the century.

Parkland Hospital's security director O. P. Wright removed the bullet from the gurney and handed it to Secret Service agent Richard Johnsen. The agent actually took the bullet with his bare hand and then slid it into his pants pocket without first photographing or preserving blood and thread evidence by placing the bullet in a proper forensic container. Add to that the problem that Darrell Tomlinson was not positive the bullet was actually found on the gurney Connally had used. Add to that the problem that Agent Johnsen and James Rowley, the Secret Service director, refused to identify the small copper-jacketed missile beyond any doubt as the FBI evidence bullet CE 399. When the

Warren Commission considered all those bad facts, it still insisted the "magic bullet" was credible evidence. With not even a chain of custody for such tainted evidence, the Texas courts would have refused to introduce the "magic bullet" as evidence for a trial.

The government's initial scenario was a three-centimeter-long (1.181-inch) copper-jacketed lead-core 6.5-millimeter rifle bullet fired from the sixth floor of the Texas School Book Depository passed through President Kennedy's neck, changed directions and traversed Governor Connally's chest, then shattered his wrist and finally embedded itself in the governor's thigh.

To have traveled through both bodies as described, this bullet traversed fifteen layers of clothing, seven layers of skin, approximately fifteen inches of tissue, struck a necktie knot, removed four inches of rib, shattered a radius bone in the forearm and finally came to rest inside a leg. Then this bullet, in almost pristine condition, became dislodged from Governor Connally's thigh, fell onto his gurney, rolled into sight from under the mat for Mr. Tomlinson to find and ended up finally being mishandled by multiple people in its journey to the Warren Commission, where it magically solved the entire assassination case. No wonder that experts in physics, ballistics, forensics and law ordained a "magical" status for such a bullet to be accepted as actual evidence by Arlen Specter.

The "single-bullet theory" was coauthored by Arlen Specter, a Philadelphia assistant district attorney (ADA), who served as the Warren Commission's assistant counsel. He arbitrarily led the Warren Commission to convert a "magic bullet," imbued with a magic theory, into an absolute fact with corrupted and reshaped medical evidence. This prevented the American people from discovering the real story and prosecuting the real murderers.

During Darrell Tomlinson's testimony before the Warren Commission, Arlen Specter had to convince him to admit there was a good possibility that he had found the bullet on Connally's stretcher. Specter had to overcome Tomlinson's growing uncertainty about who had been on the gurneys and where the gurneys had been moved. Unfortunately, the American people and the side of truth did not have an attorney present that day who would have objected to Specter leading the witness in a hostile manner. For Specter to allow Tomlinson to leave any doubt about whose gurney had produced the "magic bullet" would have left the possibility of planted evidence and a "conspiracy." Later—and absent an overbearing Arlen Specter—Tomlinson was credited with stating he highly questioned whether the gurney from which he took the bullet had anything to do with the assassination.

Later in his career as chairman of the Senate

Judiciary Committee, Arlen Specter surely knew the difference in credible evidence and magical evidence. How many Supreme Court nominees appearing before Senator Specter's committee were confirmed to the highest court through the offering of magical law theories to answer difficult and complex legal questions? What federal or state judge in America decides important cases, setting precedents based on magical and tainted evidence to shape life in America for decades? How did a man with such constitutional responsibility solve the case of who shot the president of the United States based on magical evidence?

The Warren Report was issued in September 1964, as promulgated by the President's Commission on the Assassination of President Kennedy. Arlen Specter and others connected to the Warren Commission had struggled desperately to invent a workable scenario whereby declaring Lee Harvey Oswald as the only shooting assassin. The theory would need to correlate with the Zapruder film, ballistic reports, autopsy photographs, drawings, physical evidence and the testimony from dozens of important witnesses, including Governor John Connally and his wife, Nellie. All versions and explanations making Oswald the sole gunman from behind the president's limousine were hopelessly flawed failures because Arlen Specter and the Warren Commission could not make even revamped medical evidence fit the Oswald story. Yet, the Warren Report forced round pegs through square holes and presented it to the American people as a solved crime.

In multiple meetings that produced many memorandums, the Warren Commission floated trial-balloon scenarios in its feeble attempt to explain how the wounds to President Kennedy and Governor Connally could accurately fit dozens of parameters. The different combinations of bullets and wounds had to keep time to the frames of the Zapruder film, not violate physical laws and accord with direct testimony from the witnesses. In the end, the Warren Commission simply could not rearrange the stars in the heavens. To fully explore all of their scenarios and the evidence that doomed them would exceed the pages of this book.

With so many Americans upset with the Warren Report, including Robert F. Kennedy, the United States House of Representatives Select Committee on Assassinations (HSCA) was established in 1976 to investigate the assassination of John F. Kennedy. It determined that Lee Harvey Oswald fired three shots at Kennedy. The second and third bullets from Oswald's rifle struck the president. The third shot he fired killed the president. The surprise was the HSCA admitted Oswald was not the only shooter. According to the HSCA, there were, in fact, a total of four shots fired, and that the errant bullet fired from the grassy knoll struck nothing worth noting because that bullet was never recovered.

The HSCA also agreed with the Warren Commission Report that Oswald did, in fact, fire a "magic bullet," which became the Commission's "single-bullet theory." The HSCA vaguely declared that none of their findings had to make any sense because there were just too many unknowns.

After witnessing years of destroying evidence, creating misinformation and manipulating and intimidating witnesses, the American people had finally gotten a confession that their government had lied to them about shots behind the grassy knoll and hence a conspiracy to assassinate President John F. Kennedy.

The context of the Shakespearean words "Me thinks the lady doth protest too much" was all about losing credibility when searching for truth. Dr. Crenshaw believed those exact words were appropriately relevant to the volume and intensity of the virulent protests against him—both personal and professional—for claiming the Warren Report is a fatally flawed document. The report has absolutely no credibility in its invention of a "magic bullet" as the basis to prove the Oswald assassination story. The theories advanced to fit the Oswald story lacked credibility.

Of all the detractions and criticisms levied against Dr. Crenshaw for coming forward with the medical truth about the president's wounds, the one most bogus and ridiculous was that as a third-year resident surgeon, Crenshaw was simply too young, too junior to the highest-ranking doctors in the room that November day in 1963, to have been taken seriously.

Resident physicians, more commonly and collectively referred to as "residents," are the house staff of a hospital. During their residency, they live the majority of their lives in the hospital. Residents have graduated from an accredited medical school and hold a medical degree, with many having completed their internship. Duration of most residencies can range from three years to seven years for a specialized field, such as neurosurgery. Dr. Crenshaw had served his internship at the Veterans Administration Hospital and was in his third year of a five-year residency at Parkland.

Dr. Crenshaw was one of six doctors in Trauma Room 1 to use a scalpel on President Kennedy. He performed a cutdown on the president's right leg to expose surgically the saphenous vein to insert a catheter for Ringer's lactate (RL) solution to flow into the president's body. Would the senior doctors have allowed anyone but a superlative physician and surgeon to perform that surgical procedure on the president of the United States?

In fact, Dr. Crenshaw's participation in Trauma Room 1 is tantamount proof that Dr. Crenshaw performing such critical procedures in the emergency area of Parkland Hospital was not an unusual occurrence at all. Dr. Crenshaw's participation that day in that room to treat President Kennedy was in keeping with Dr. Crenshaw's regular duties as a physician and surgeon—and not anomalous simply because he was one of the doctors who converged on Trauma Room 1, as some critics and detractors on the periphery have suggested.

Save Dr. Kemp Clark, there was not one of the high-ranking doctors willing to take charge and pronounce a dead president "dead." Even with a critical portion of President Kennedy's brains blown from two holes in his skull, not one senior doctor would take charge and give Dr. Rose an opportunity to gather the evidence that would have answered the questions that now plague history. So what possible advantage was there in having doctors senior to Dr. Crenshaw in the room to treat President Kennedy?

Many times a professional will rise unexpectedly from obscurity and do something incredible and surprising. For example, average soldiers sometimes rise from the ranks of their fellow comrades—to the surprise of their superior officers—and perform unusual heroics to win the Congressional Medal of Honor. Such heroics are usually performed when there is collective reluctance by others to act assertively. For twenty-nine years, the doctors in Trauma Room 1 had been frozen in collective reticence to proclaim the truth, in part because of Dr. Baxter's threat.

Dr. Crenshaw was on the front line of doctors in the battle at Parkland Hospital to save both President Kennedy and Lee Harvey Oswald. There is documentation that proves those facts beyond any question or doubt. And it was Dr. Crenshaw who finally sprang from the collective reticence and obscurity of the other doctors, and defied the Baxter edict to (1) proclaim in a comprehensive work that the autopsy photographs prove President Kennedy's wounds were altered, (2) declared the autopsy by Dr. James J. Humes a sham and a fraud and (3) said the Warren Commission Report with its "single-bullet theory" was a lie. For such gall and courage to take on the Warren Commission and the powers behind it, Dr. Crenshaw is entitled to be awarded posthumously a Medal of Honor for medicine.

Acknowledgments

Bob Gill is currently serving as deputy director of the criminal division of the Tarrant

County Criminal District Attorney's Office. He previously served as judge of the 213th District Court of Tarrant County, presiding over felony criminal cases from January 1, 1993, until he retired on May 31, 2007. He is a graduate of the University of Illinois and the Southern Illinois University School of Law. Before taking the bench, Judge Gill served eleven years as an assistant criminal district attorney in Tarrant County.

Judge Gill has been board certified in criminal law since 1988. He is a member of the State Bar of Texas and the Tarrant County Bar Association. He has served Tarrant County as presiding criminal judge and juvenile board chairman and twice served as the local administrative judge of Tarrant County. Judge Gill has written and lectured extensively on criminal law topics. He is the author of *The Texas Criminal Lawyers Handbook* and *Texas Criminal Forms*, both published by James Publishing.

2

THE *TRUE* FABRICATORS

ARE EXPOSED

J. Gary Shaw

When Dr. Charles Crenshaw undertook the writing of *JFK: Conspiracy of Silence,* he was given fair warning by me, his coauthor J. Gary Shaw. He was told that the forces that would align against him would be more powerful and determined than he could imagine, and that they would be without mercy. He indicated that he was prepared for the challenge. However, after the book, the controversy, and a lawsuit, Charles Crenshaw would later admit that he had not—indeed could not—have grasped the sound and the fury the first book from inside Parkland's Trauma Room 1 had generated.

Crenshaw was shocked and hurt when he discovered that he was the target of "friendly fire," criticism and insults from some of the other Parkland doctors who had attended JFK at Parkland Memorial twenty-nine years earlier. Crenshaw had always been proud of Parkland Hospital and of the surgeons it produced.

He felt that the men who had worked on Kennedy's body with him would be pleased that he had told his story, for he felt this was their story as well. They had worked together. They had seen Kennedy's wounds. They all would agree with him, or so Crenshaw thought. After over a quarter of a century, it was time, and he was breaking the conspiracy of silence for them all.

But there was a storm brewing. Oliver Stone's *JFK* was in theaters and was having an impact. There were demands for immediate release of withheld government files and for another investigation. Now, along comes Crenshaw, not just a witness but a participant, a trained medical man who had seen Kennedy's body within minutes of the time the president was shot. Crenshaw was saying that, based on what he saw in Trauma Room 1, Kennedy was hit by two bullets fired at him from the front. *JFK: Conspiracy of Silence* sold and, in fact, became a best-selling paperback.

Crenshaw was on national television, articulate and comfortable, telling what he and the other Parkland doctors had seen. Their observations were what could be called "pure" medical evidence. Crenshaw and his colleagues had no foreknowledge, no prior theories, no concepts of grassy knolls, book depositories, what witnesses in Dealey Plaza had seen or heard. As far as they knew, JFK could have been shot in a phone booth. They met the requirements for excellent witnesses: educated, trained, without preconceptions, and with ample opportunity to observe JFK's wounded body. (In his book *Case Closed*, Gerald Posner attempted to downplay the findings of the Parkland doctors, claiming they were too involved in trying to save the president's life to make careful examination and form opinions. However, a reading of their written reports, which were made just hours after Kennedy's body was carried out of the emergency room, shows that they made careful and accurate observations. (Dr. Robert McClelland, who held a retractor in JFK's neck, looked into the back of JFK's head at a distance of two feet or less for over twenty minutes, doing nothing else in that time.) Not a single Parkland doctor responded to questions by Posner or other investigators by saying that they could not see the wounds, were not in a position to comment about the wounds, or would prefer not to speculate on the wounds.

So Crenshaw had to be stopped. The silence had to begin again. The upstart doctor had to be punished. George Lundberg, then editor of the *Journal of the American Medical Association* (*JAMA*), assigned Dennis Breo, a veteran *JAMA* reporter, to put Charles Crenshaw in his place before this whole "breaking the silence" thing got out of hand.

Exactly who assigned (ordered?) Lundberg

to initiate this politically—*not* medically—focused attack is still unclear. One thing, however, is crystal clear; the force behind the attack was not a foreign entity.

JAMA's May 27, 1992, issue published two articles dealing with medical aspects of the assassination of President John F. Kennedy. The first of these two articles drew on interviews with two of the attending military autopsy pathologists, Dr. James J. Humes and Dr. J. Thornton Boswell. The second article, "Dallas MDs Recall Their Memories," was said to be based upon interviews with Dallas doctors who participated in the treatment of President Kennedy at Parkland Memorial Hospital just minutes after he was shot. Both *JAMA* articles contained attacks on Dr. Crenshaw and the book *JFK: Conspiracy of Silence.*

In the original of this book, Dr. Crenshaw had stated:

1. He participated in the treatment of President John F. Kennedy at Parkland Hospital.
2. He observed both Kennedy's head wound and throat wound, and his medical judgment was that both wounds resulted from shots that struck President Kennedy from the front.
3. Autopsy photographs that were shown to Dr. Crenshaw, which were said to depict the two

wounds, were incompatible with the nature and location of the wounds he saw in the emergency room.

4. Many of Dr. Crenshaw's Dallas colleagues reported the wounds to be in the same location and to be of the same nature that he had observed.

5. He participated in the treatment of Lee Harvey Oswald on Sunday, November 24, when Oswald was brought to Parkland.

6. While Oswald was being treated, Dr. Crenshaw was called to a telephone in the operating room, where he talked with President Lyndon B. Johnson, who told him that there was a person present in the operating room to take a deathbed confession from Oswald.

Dr. Crenshaw was both hurt and angered by the attacks on his credibility in the *JAMA* articles. He considered them to be distortions of the facts. If the irresponsible author of the *JAMA* articles had turned to the previous statements of the Dallas doctors he interviewed, he would have found that those statements contradicted what they were telling him, and that, in fact, their previous statements—contemporaneous and under oath—actually supported Dr. Crenshaw's description of the president's wounds. The official record devastates the points *JAMA* attempted to make.

Parkland Hospital

Friday afternoon, November 22, 1963

Just after 12:40 P.M. on Friday, November 22, Dr. Crenshaw entered Trauma Room 1 at Parkland Hospital with Dr. Bob McClelland. Several other Parkland doctors were already there. President Kennedy lay, mortally wounded, on a stretcher. For the next several minutes, Crenshaw helped administrate emergency treatment to the president, and he observed both his throat wound and the wound at the right rear of his head.

He then helped remove President Kennedy's trousers and, with Dr. Ken Salyer, proceeded to perform a cutdown and insert an IV catheter, which fed Ringer's lactate solution into Kennedy's right leg. At the same time, other Parkland doctors were performing a tracheostomy, inserting chest tubes, and doing a similar cutdown on the left leg. Two wounds were visible. There was a small, round opening in the front of the midline of the throat. This became the site of Dr. Malcolm Perry's tracheostomy incision. In the occipitoparietal region at the right rear of the head, there was an avulsive (torn-away) wound nearly as large as a fist. Bone, scalp and hair were missing in the region, and brain tissue, including much of the cerebellum, was hanging from the opening. Dr. Crenshaw considered the throat wound to be an entrance wound and the large head wound to be an exit wound. Along with many of his Parkland colleagues, he believed at the time that President Kennedy had been hit twice from the front. He believed that until the day he died.

Writing with what must have been minimal research, the author of the *JAMA* article had the audacity to question whether or not Dr. Crenshaw was even present in Trauma Room 1. At one point, the author wrote, *Crenshaw, who was a surgical resident in 1963, is not mentioned in the Warren Commission's 888-page summary report.... * At another point, he wrote, *Since it is hard to prove a negative, no one can say with certainty what some suspect—that Crenshaw was not even in the trauma room, none of the four [Parkland doctors interviewed by the author] recalls ever seeing him at the scene.*

In actual fact, Dr. Crenshaw's presence in Trauma Room 1 was noted in sworn testimony before the Warren Commission eight times by five different doctors and nurses who saw him there. Dr. Charles Baxter, who apparently told *JAMA* he could not recall seeing him there, stated in his Warren Commission testimony that Crenshaw was there! So did Dr. Robert "Bob" McClelland, who entered the room with him. Dr. Don Curtis and Nurse Margaret Hinchcliffe also testified that Dr. Crenshaw was present. Dr. Ken Salyer, who worked with him on the President's IV, told the Commission he was there participating "about the extent that I did."

The record makes it amply clear that Dr. Crenshaw was in Trauma Room 1 doing precisely what he wrote in *JFK: Conspiracy of Silence.* Why, then, did the *JAMA* article make these innuendos? In light of the misrepresentations and outright falsehoods revealed in the article, one must conclude that a major purpose for the May 1992 articles was to discredit Charles Crenshaw, and that their author and editor either chose not to check the official record—or elected to ignore what they found there.

The White House Telephone Call

In *JFK: Conspiracy of Silence,* Dr. Crenshaw told of being on duty at Parkland when Lee Harvey Oswald was brought there, and of assisting with Oswald's treatment. While he was in the room, he observed a large man in a scrub suit, with a gun visible in his pocket. He believed the man to be some sort of government agent. Crenshaw handed him a sterile mask. At one point, a nurse tapped Dr. Crenshaw on the shoulder and asked him to take a telephone call. In an adjoining office, he talked with President Johnson, who told him that they should try to get a confession from Oswald and that a person was present for the purpose of taking a confession. In an attempt to refute this, *JAMA* quoted Dr. Baxter: *"Did that happen? Heavens no . . . imagine that, the president of the United States personally calls for Charles Crenshaw."*

It did happen and there is ample proof. It should first be noted that Dr. Crenshaw *never* claimed that President Johnson called for him personally. He was simply tapped on the shoulder by a nurse to take the call. The call did occur:

1. Dr. Phillip E. Williams, Dallas neurosurgeon, was quoted in the New York Times: *"I vividly remember someone said . . . the White House is calling and President Johnson wants to know what the status of Oswald is. I heard the statement in the operating room, and it was not Dr. Crenshaw's book or anyone else who revived my thoughts about this because I have said this for years."*

2. Phyllis Bartlett was the chief telephone operator at Parkland Hospital that day. She definitely remembers taking the call from a man who identified himself as President Johnson, then transferring the call to the operating room.

3. The presence of federal agents in the operating room is also well documented. Alex Rosen, assistant director of the FBI, was ordered by Director Hoover to get a man to Parkland to get a statement from the accused assassin. Rosen stated that he had contacted Forrest Sorrels, of the Dallas Secret Service office. Sorrels said an agent was already there.

The time was 12:18 P.M. in Dallas. The *Dallas Times-Herald* of Sunday, December 22, 1963, carried a story that an agent wearing hospital clothing and a surgical mask had waited in vain for a confession from Oswald. In response to this, the Dallas FBI's new (he had just been transferred to Dallas in April) Special Agent in Charge (SAIC) J. Gordon Shanklin sent an Airtel to Hoover that stated in part: *SA Charles T. Brown and SA Wallace R. Heitman made arrangements . . . to be available in the event Oswald regained consciousness. In order to save time and be immediately available, these agents did don operating clothing and took positions outside the operating room.*

However, the agents did enter the room. Dr. Paul Peters, who was present and attending Oswald, said: "There were Secret Service men intermingled with the operating-room personnel. . . . Some were dressed in green clothes as the surgeons. . . . Two or three shouted in his ear, 'Did you do it? Did you do it?'"

Once again, the *JAMA* articles are incorrect. There is clear and convincing evidence of both the White House telephone call and the presence of federal agents in the operating room— precisely as Dr. Crenshaw stated.

The President's Wounds

There was no doubt in Dr. Crenshaw's mind that the attacks on him by a professional journal were occasioned by his assertion that President Kennedy's wounds indicated to a doctor present on the scene that he had been shot from the front, which, of course, meant a conspiracy. The wound he saw in President Kennedy's throat was clearly a smooth and rounded entry wound. The wound in the right rear of the head, both in its location and its nature, must have been inflicted from the front. As Dr. Crenshaw stated, his conclusion in Trauma Room 1 was that these wounds were made by two shots striking President Kennedy from the front. That was his firm conclusion. And the official record—ignored by *JAMA*—shows that he was not alone in those conclusions.

JAMA talked with several of the Parkland doctors about their experiences and Dr. Crenshaw's book. Charles James "Jim" Carrico, Marion T. "Pepper" Jenkins, Charles Baxter and Malcolm Perry were interviewed. In spite of the fact that the *JAMA* author visited in Dallas, he made absolutely no effort to contact Dr. Crenshaw or to get his side of the story. All four of his former colleagues are quoted as having condemned Crenshaw's conclusions about shots from the front and asserted that what they saw in Trauma Room 1 was completely compatible with the autopsy photographs, as well as the autopsy findings, which concluded that Kennedy was shot twice from the rear, not from the front.

As *JAMA* presented it, this was a case of four Dallas doctors standing firmly against

Dr. Charles Crenshaw, sensationalist. These doctors, if quoted correctly by *JAMA*, seemed to question everything from motive to sanity. Dr. Baxter is said to have stated that the only motive he could find for Crenshaw was a "desire for personal recognition" and "monetary gain"; Dr. Perry said that Crenshaw was on TV saying this "bogus stuff to reach out for his day in the sun"; Dr. Carrico apparently decided that Crenshaw had dreams of grandeur; while the article quoted Dr. Jenkins as saying, *"Crenshaw's conclusions are dead wrong."*

Was Dr. Crenshaw outnumbered? No, not at all. His strongest ally went unmentioned by *JAMA*. His strongest ally is the record—the official record—the statements made by Drs. Perry, Baxter, Carrico and Jenkins long before they ever talked to *JAMA*. The strongest "witnesses" against *JAMA* and the four Dallas doctors are the doctors themselves!

The previous official statements of these four doctors, which we will now examine, come from statements written by many Parkland doctors within two to three hours of having attended President Kennedy. Many of these are handwritten and are of immense significance. They represent the first accounts of President Kennedy's wounds based on observation by trained medical personnel and "pure" medical data. That is, when Drs. Perry, Baxter, Jenkins, Carrico and others wrote their statements on Friday afternoon, they had no knowledge of "single-bullet theory," Lee Harvey Oswald, the grassy knoll, the School Book Depository or other evidentiary factors to affect opinions. They also stand as the only recorded medical opinions about Kennedy's wounds before the body was forcibly and illegally (by gunpoint) taken from Dallas by the Secret Service.

These doctor's statements are found in the Warren Report, Appendix VIII, and should be read by any person who is genuinely interested in knowing where President Kennedy was shot. It is a shame that the *JAMA* author and his editor didn't read them before Breo went to Dallas and interviewed the four doctors.

In addition to these earliest observations, all four doctors testified under oath before the Warren Commission in March 1964, and three of them (Carrico, Jenkins and Perry) were deposed, again under oath, by the House Select Committee on Assassinations (HSCA) in 1977.

When we examine the four doctors' previous statements, we find that, instead of refuting Dr. Crenshaw's observations, they actually support them.

Dr. Perry and Kennedy's Head Wound

Within hours of seeing President Kennedy's body, Malcolm Perry described the head wound as "a large wound of the right posterior cranium." Four months later, in testimony before the Warren Commission, Perry would call it "a large avulsive wound of the right occipitoparietal area" and noted that "both scalp and portions of the skull were absent. . . ." In his deposition for the HSCA, Perry stated that "the parietal occipital head wound was largely avulsive."

These three references to the head wound are clearly consistent with each other. But, as can be clearly seen, they are also clearly consistent with Dr. Crenshaw's description of the head wound, both in its location and its appearance.

DR. PERRY AND THE CEREBELLUM

When Malcolm Perry gave his HSCA deposition, he stated: "There was visible brain tissue in the macard [*sic*] and some cerebellum was seen." Both Malcolm Perry and Dr. Crenshaw saw cerebellar tissue in the head wound.

Dr. Perry and the Throat Wound

Malcolm Perry was in a unique position to observe the wound in the midline of the throat. He made the tracheostomy incision through that throat wound and inserted a tracheostomy tube. Within an hour of President Kennedy's death, Dr. Perry described Kennedy's wounds to newsmen. A transcript of the press conference exists; and in his statements, Dr. Perry identified *three times* the throat wound he had just seen as an "entrance wound."

By the following day, evidence had emerged suggesting that the shots that struck Kennedy had come from the Texas School Book Depository above and behind him. Nonetheless, Dr. Perry spoke to a *Boston Globe* reporter, Herbert Black, and continued to maintain that a bullet had entered the front of the throat. It is clear that on the weekend of the assassination, Malcolm Perry apparently was convinced that the wound in the president's throat was an entrance wound—and said so.

Dr. Jenkins and Kennedy's Head Wound

In his written statement, dated 4:30 P.M., three and a half hours after seeing the president's wounds, Dr. Jenkins described: *great laceration of the right side of the head (temporal and occipital).* Fourteen years later, he told the HSCA: "One segment of bone was blown out— this was a segment of occipital or temporal bone."

Dr. Jenkins saw the same wound Dr. Crenshaw saw—and described it in the same way.

DR. JENKINS AND THE CEREBELLUM

Jenkins also describes "herniation and laceration of great areas of the brain, even to the extent that the cerebellum had protruded from the wound." In March, four months later, he testified under oath, "Part of the brain was herniated. I really think part of the cerebellum . . . was hanging out of the wound." Fourteen years after the assassination, when Jenkins was deposed by the HSCA, he stated that he "noted that a portion of the cerebellum was hanging out from a hole in the right-rear of the head."

And what is *JAMA*'s comment about Jenkins and the cerebellum? *Dr. Jenkins wrote in a 1963 report that Kennedy's "cerebellum" had been blown out when he meant "cerebrum."*

However, a study of the record shows that Jenkins wrote "cerebellum"—*not* "cerebrum"— on the day of the assassination. He swore to this before the Warren Commission four months later, then swore to it again fourteen years later to the HSCA!

Dr. Carrico and Kennedy's Head Wound

Dr. Carrico was the first Parkland doctor to enter Trauma Room 1. A few hours later, he wrote a description of the head wound he saw. Carrico recorded, *The other wound had avulsed the calvarium and shredded brain tissue present and profuse oozing.* In his Warren Commission testimony, he located the wound more specifically: "I saw a large gaping wound located in the right occipitoparietal area." And Carrico told HSCA there was a "fairly large wound in the right side of the head, in the parietal, occipital area. . . . That wound [would] be above and posterior to the ear."

DR. CARRICO AND THE CEREBELLUM

In his Warren Commission testimony, Carrico said, "The skull was fragmented and bleeding cerebral and cerebellar tissue." At another point in his questioning, he said, "I believe there was shredded macerated cerebral and cerebellar tissue both in the wounds and on the fragments of skull attached to the dura." In his 1977 HSCA deposition, Carrico stated, "One could see blood and brains, both cerebrum and cerebellum fragments in that wound."

Dr. Carrico and the Throat Wound

In his statement on Friday afternoon, in describing the president's throat wound, Carrico wrote: [there was] *one small penetrating wound of mid-neck in lower ⅓.*

Dr. Baxter and Kennedy's Head Wound

On the afternoon of the assassination, Dr. Baxter wrote, *The rt [sic] temporal and occipital bones were missing the brain was lying on the table.*

DR. BAXTER AND THE CEREBELLUM

Dr. Baxter testified that "the cerebellum was present—a large quantity of the brain was present on the cart."

Dr. Baxter and the Throat Wound

When he testified before the Warren Commission, Baxter conceded that the throat wound could have been either an entrance wound or an exit wound. But his other statements about the wound are enlightening: "This wound was, in my estimation, four to five millimeters in widest diameter and was a spherical wound . . . so that it was . . . very small." Also, "Judging from the caliber of the rifle that we later found or became acquainted with, this would more resemble a wound of entry."

These are the statements, nearly all of them official, of the four Dallas doctors, formerly colleagues, who ridiculed Dr. Crenshaw and his claims in *JAMA*. In summary: (1) Dr. Crenshaw saw a wound in the back of the head—occipital and parietal. So did Jenkins, Carrico, Baxter and Perry. Some say "occipital" and "parietal"; others say "occipital" and "temporal." The occipital bone in the rear of the head is mentioned by all of them. The size and nature of the wound is very similar in all our descriptions; (2) Dr. Crenshaw saw cerebellar tissue hanging out of the large head wound. So did Jenkins, Carrico, Baxter and Perry; (3) Dr. Crenshaw saw a small entrance wound in the front of the throat. Perry called it an "entrance wound"; Carrico called it a "penetrating wound." Baxter still says it could have been an entrance wound.

Other Dallas Doctors

Many other Parkland doctors were present in Trauma Room 1, and they, too, wrote statements and testified before the Warren Commission. Their statements further bolster Dr. Crenshaw's claims.

THE HEAD WOUND

Dr. Kemp Clark saw "two external wounds . . . the other in the occipital area of the skull . . . a large wound of the occipitoparietal area."

Dr. Paul Peters "noted that there was a large defect in the occiput."

Dr. Ronald Jones reported, "There was a large defect in the back of the head."

Dr. Gene Coleman Akin stated, "In the back of the right occipitoparietal, part of the skull was shattered."

Dr. Robert McClelland "noted that the right posterior portion of the skull had been extremely blasted. . . . Some of the occipital bone was fractured in its lateral half."

CEREBELLAR TISSUE

Dr. Kemp Clark said, "Both cerebral and cerebellar tissue were extruding from the wound."

THE THROAT WOUND

Dr. Paul Peters noted, "We saw the wound of entry in the throat and noted the large occipital wound."

Dr. Ronald Jones stated that "a small hole in the midline of the neck [was] thought to be a bullet entrance wound."

Again with these doctors, we see the consistent "Dallas pattern"—small, round wound in the front of the throat, large hole opening backward in the right rear of the head, and cerebral and cerebellar tissue hanging from the skull. It was clear that their observations were the same as Dr. Crenshaw's—that two of the bullets that struck President Kennedy were fired from the front.

What Dr. Crenshaw saw in the emergency room at Parkland Hospital forced him to disagree with the Bethesda autopsy report, which concluded that the president was hit by two bullets, which were "fired from a point behind and somewhat above the level of the deceased." It is alarming that the four doctors interviewed by *JAMA* said they saw nothing that contradicted that "official" finding.

The Autopsy Photographs

Dr. Crenshaw also found great problems with the autopsy photographs. He stated that any photograph that showed a completely intact skull at a point where he saw a hole nearly the size of his fist was wrong. Any photograph, he said, that did not show cerebellar tissue shredded and hanging from that hole was illegitimate. There was no way that he could reconcile the autopsy photographs with the wounds he saw on John F. Kennedy's body in Trauma Room 1 at Parkland on November 22, 1963. Dr. Crenshaw was amazed and greatly troubled by the fact that *JAMA* reported how his former colleagues said they could do so.

The four doctors who commented to *JAMA* are reported to have found no problem with the photographs, in spite of the fact that they obviously show a head wound of a different size in a totally different location than the one they saw and reported on November 22.

Photographs of the Throat Wound

Several autopsy photographs show what is alleged to be the tracheostomy incision that Dr. Malcolm Perry made through a bullet hole in Kennedy's neck. When Dr. Crenshaw first saw these photos, he was shocked at the size and character of the defect there. According to the autopsy report, the incision measured 6.5 centimeters (2.56 inches) in length. When Dr. Humes testified before the Warren Commission, he placed the length of the defect at seven to eight centimeters (2.75 to 3.15 inches).

The wound that Dr. Crenshaw saw in Trauma Room 1—*after* Dr. Perry completed his work—looked nothing like what he saw in the photographs allegedly taken at Bethesda. Dr. Perry had made a small and very neat transverse incision, which Dr. Crenshaw took to be about 1 to 1½ inches in length, and it was certainly not of the length he saw in the autopsy photos. The gaping nature of the wound was also totally inconsistent with what he saw. When the body left Parkland, there was no gaping, bloody defect in the front of the throat, just the small bullet hole and the thin line of Perry's precise incision.

According to the *JAMA* article, the four Dallas doctors had no problem in reconciling the autopsy photos with the tracheostomy incision they observed: *"I was right there and the tracheostomy I observed and the autopsy photos look the same—very compatible,"* Dr. Baxter was quoted as having said. Dr. Carrico said, *"I've seen the autopsy photos and they are very compatible to the actual tracheostomy."*

"They are the same" is the comment attributed to Dr. Jenkins. Dr. Perry qualified his response: *"Of course, tissues sag and stretch after death, but any suggestion that this wound was intentionally enlarged is wrong."*

Once again, however, there is a previous

record. In 1966, three of these doctors estimated the length of the incision Perry made in Kennedy's throat. Their responses were recorded by a researcher. Dr. Carrico said it was "between two and three centimeters—which is close to an inch." Dr. Perry, who made the incision, estimated it at "two to three centimeters" (.787 to 1.181 inches), while Dr. Baxter remembered it as "roughly an inch and a half."

Twenty-six years later, in 1992, these men were said to believe that there was no contradiction between what they originally saw and the 6.5- to 8-centimeter (2⅝ inch to 3¼ inch) gaping gash shown in the autopsy photographs.

Dr. Crenshaw saw that incision. He also saw the occipitoparietal head wound. When he was shown alleged autopsy photographs that depict wounds that differ so markedly from those he saw at Parkland, he had no choice but to conclude that someone had gone to a great deal of trouble to present a different story than they had seen at Parkland. The result of those wound differences caused the body of President Kennedy to appear more like it had been shot from the rear—not like it was shot from the front.

Observing the Head Wound

The *JAMA* article sought to minimize the significance of what the doctors saw in Dallas by implying that they were occupied with lifesaving measures and did not have an opportunity to look at the head wound carefully: *In fact, Dr. Jenkins doubts if any of the Parkland physicians even had a good look at the President's head. . . .*

Once again, though, there's that pesky record: Dr. Kemp Clark said he "examined the wound in the back of the president's head." Dr. Robert McClelland stated, "As I took the position at the head of the table, I was in such a position that I could very closely examine the head wound." Dr. Jenkins was interviewed for an article in the *American Medical News* in 1978. In that article, he said: *"It may be that I and Malcolm Perry (MD) [sic] were the first ones aware of the head injury. We were standing at the patient's head and with that thick shock of hair, when he was lying supine on the stretcher, it really didn't show that he had part of his head blown away and part of his cerebellum was hanging out."*

This, once again, pinpoints the location of the wound at the rear of the head. Note also that in 1978, Dr. Jenkins still recalled the cerebellum—supposedly undamaged—as being blown out of the wound.

There is ample evidence that these doctors, as well as Dr. Crenshaw, did see the head wound. It is a simple fact that nearly every Dallas doctor, while under oath, was asked by the Warren Commission where the head wound was located. And each of the doctors placed the wound in the back of Kennedy's head. Not one of them said he did not know, could not remember or did not have an opportunity to observe.

Without ever having talked with Dr. Crenshaw, *JAMA* editor Dr. George Lundberg called the book *JFK: Conspiracy of Silence*, "a sad fabrication based on unsubstantiated allegations." In contrast, he proclaimed the *JAMA* article to be information that was "scientifically sound," furnished "the definitive history of what happened" and provided "irrefutable proof that President Kennedy was killed by two bullets that struck him from above and behind." The record, however, indicates otherwise. The reader can determine who has produced a sad fabrication based upon unsubstantiated allegations—and who the true fabricators were. The record, standing in stark contrast to the statements the four doctors are quoted as having made in the May 1992 *JAMA* article, will not go away.

What a horrible and alarming injustice that *JAMA* preferred to disregard that record blatantly and outrageously.

Unlawful Seizure and Polluted Pathology

Author and JFK researcher David Lifton fired the first powerful volley in the modern inquiry into the location and significance of President Kennedy's wounds. His 1981 book, *Best Evidence*, argued that the wounds on Kennedy's body had been surgically altered from the defects that the Parkland doctors had seen and interpreted as entrance wounds. The purpose of this alteration was to change the alleged trajectories of the bullets that killed him. Lifton's painstaking research showed how the body's wrappings and even the caskets used in transporting his corpse had changed after the Secret Service took the body—illegally and by force—from the morgue at Parkland Memorial Hospital before Dr. Earl Rose, an accomplished forensic pathologist, could have performed the autopsy required by Texas law. Lifton's book caused so much controversy that *Time* magazine reviewed it, not in the "books" section, but in its section on "National News."

Few Americans even today know of this confrontation in the corridors of Parkland Hospital within the hour of Kennedy's death. It was, to say the least, a surreal scene: Roy Kellerman and his team of Secret Service agents, with automatic weapons drawn, cursing and pushing the casket—not to the morgue for the autopsy, but toward the exit doors leading to a hearse, to *Air Force One* at Love Field, then to a military hospital in Maryland. Other people affected and on hand: Jackie Kennedy, her pink Chanel suit spattered with her husband's blood;

Father Oscar Huber, trying to escort the casket after having just administered the Last Rites of the Catholic Church; Aubrey Rike, a driver for the O'Neal Funeral Home & Ambulance Service of Fort Worth, the front of his shirt stained with Kennedy's blood, smeared there as he had helped to put the president's body into a casket in Trauma Room 1 just minutes before; and Earl Rose, the agitated coroner, trying to move the body to the place where Texas law required it go—the morgue, just a short distance below. The federal agents would not be denied. Rike struggled to try to hold the crucifix atop the shifting casket being tugged at by so many hands. He remembered his embarrassment that the widowed first lady, standing beside him, and the priest had to listen to the profanities filling the corridor.

Later, Kellerman's men (and their bosses) would offer an explanation for their actions on that afternoon. Johnson was at *Air Force One*, waiting to be sworn in, and he wanted to return to Washington immediately as a symbol of control and continuity of government in this unprecedented crisis. LBJ did not want to leave the slain president's body behind in Dallas. Jackie wanted to be with her husband's body. All these things made persuasive and emotional arguments for the Secret Service's actions.

But Lifton's book (and the research it has triggered) put a different light on the events in that Parkland corridor. It is clear now that JFK's body did not make an uninterrupted journey to the Bethesda National Navy Medical Center from Dallas. It left in one casket and arrived in another, left in hospital wrapping and arrived in a body bag.

And, far more significant, the wounds observed on the body changed during this illegal odyssey. The wounds seen by Dr. Crenshaw and the trained medical personnel in Trauma Room 1 had been enlarged and shifted, so much so that one of the autopsy doctors who was so hastily (and ill-advisedly) chosen to perform the illegal autopsy at Bethesda exclaimed that there had been surgery to the top of Kennedy's head. No surgery of the head was done in Dallas. The body had traveled fifteen hundred miles from Dallas to Bethesda; the wounds had traveled a few inches. This would drive the JFK discussion for the next half century.

The medical issues continue to be discussed with heat and vigor. But one thing is certain: If Texas law had been followed, if Earl Rose had performed the autopsy, there would be no controversy over where Kennedy was shot (what direction, what trajectories, what ammunition) and, knowing those facts, who shot him. And that is the real reason the autopsy could not be allowed to occur in Dallas—the real stimulus for the absurd scene that stands as one of the key pieces of the Kennedy puzzle.

David Lifton often said that changing the wounds in this (or any other shooting) was like polluting a river at its very source. Everything that flows downstream from this source—the water and the evidence—is contaminated and falsified. We have seen this constantly on our TV screens in the past two decades. Using the wound pattern depicted in photographs placed in the National Archives, computer experts and their software build cyber-Dealey Plazas, cyber-JFKs and cyber-Connallys. They shoot melons, carcasses and skins, eject "blood" of every hue, and then proclaim that their cyber/laser technology shows that the shots that day, fifty years ago, originated from . . . (drumroll) . . . the sixth floor of the Texas School Book Depository.

What these latter-day assassination gurus do not tell you is that the photos and X-rays that they are using to "prove" where the shots came from *do not agree* with what people *who actually saw* JFK's body at Parkland and at Bethesda saw. Not one person. The visuals they are using depict "evidence" never seen by any living person. The medical truth was replaced when JFK's body was snatched from Parkland Hospital by force. What we have is the stuff produced, as Lifton said, by polluting the evidence at its source. And it has been used too long to fabricate a false story of the shooting on Kennedy's body and the autopsy photos.

Fake the Facts to Maintain the Myth

On several occasions prior to his death, Dr. Crenshaw and I had discussed various aspects of the JFK case. We both agreed that the exact *how* of the assassination would probably never be known; despite several spurious, make-believe investigations and inquiries, there was just simply too much we didn't know about the shooting.

Furthermore, we had determined that at this late date there were things we could never know about the crime and cover-up. As it now stood, we surmised, the probative value of the evidence was nil. However, despite this fact, the Warren Commission apologists continued their effort to force-feed the lie of the lone assassin to a very skeptical public. And, though it hasn't worked for the last forty-nine years—and will never work—the purveyors of this shameful and deceitful account of this national tragedy just keep on coming.

Garbage In, Garbage Out

There's an old saying "What you don't know won't hurt you." Truth is, though, what you don't know (or worse, refuse to acknowledge) can hurt you. And this certainly applies to the Discovery and NatGeo television networks in the making of their respective JFK assassination documentaries. Perhaps even more pertinent to their productions is the "computer age" saying "Garbage in, garbage out." This expression is computer slang for the idea that putting erroneous data into a computer will always give erroneous results. This idea is certainly applicable to the presentations of the Discovery Channel and National Geographic television networks in their feeble and futile attempts to replicate the shooting of President Kennedy. In these instances, the garbage, which was fed in and spewed out, was dangerous, malignant and contaminating. These documentaries could have been informative and enlightening, had their use of "creative license" in regard to the shooting sequence, bullet trajectories and the victim's wounds not been so erroneous and despicably jerry-rigged by their so-called experts. When no legitimate and credible evidence is available—because none exists—that's not a problem. . . . Create your own!

The Discovery Channel's *JFK: Inside the Target Car* came out in 2008 with the boastful claim that "Tech Snuffs JFK Conspiracy." The show's producers proclaimed to one and all that the "fateful day has been re-created by technology experts" and that "Oswald shot and killed the president."

NatGeo aired their documentary *JFK: The Lost Bullet* in 2011. Their promise to prospective viewers was to "expose the hidden secrets of the crime of the century." Their findings came as no surprise; the Warren Commission was right all along and the much-maligned "single-bullet theory" was correct. NatGeo's self-styled authorities magically created the necessary analysis that enabled them to invent a bullet trajectory that satisfied the criteria for the government's lone-assassin scenario. Forget all the half-truths, untruths, suppression of evidence, creation of evidence and imagination required to perform this feat. After all, it's the results that count.

Were the re-creations and conclusions of these documentaries even close to fact? The answer is an emphatic NO! *Fact* must be founded on *real* knowledge and *real* information, and this kind of evidence is virtually non-existent in this case. Therefore, both networks were forced to depend on the corrupted, conflicting and unreliable evidence provided by the government's heavily flawed investigations. It was garbage in, garbage out!

With these considerations in mind, how does one go about duplicating the shooting that occurred in Dealey Plaza? *The simple truth, and the answer to that question, is that an informed and honest investigator and/or producer* must *admit up-front that it can't be done*. The *why* it can't be done is simple. However, the *reason* as to *why* it can't be done is much more complex.

The reason as to *why* a replication of the shooting is no longer possible is because most, if not all, of the accurate and dependable evidence pertaining to the crime is no longer available. *Why* it is no longer available is directly due to the malfeasance (whether by ineptness or design—or both) of the responsible authorities. It was their fault; it was their actions or inactions that have rendered the ballistic evidence, the medical evidence and the crime scene evidence untrustworthy—so much so that it would not be admissible in any legitimate court in the land.

With few, if any, exceptions, each and every piece of evidence in the case has been so thoroughly corrupted, tainted, lost, manipulated or destroyed that any attempt to investigate and re-create the crime is completely impossible; and any and all results of such an attempt would have absolutely no validity whatsoever. And *anyone* who says otherwise is either totally ignorant of the true facts in the case, is a disinformation specialist, is a liar or has a vested interest in the perpetuation of the myth of a sole assassin and no conspiracy.

Substantiation of this statement is found in a brief examination of each of the three evidentiary areas mentioned above. In highlighting what we don't know about these areas, we can pinpoint just why it is impossible for anyone to replicate the shooting scenario realistically and accurately.

First, there's the ballistic evidence. Because the medico-legal aspects of the case were so botched and manipulated, there no longer exists the ability to ascertain the number and direction of the shots. Without knowing exactly how many shots actually struck the victims (we don't), and without accurate, reliable information to track the bullet path into and through the victim (we can't), the missile's trajectory and point of origin can *never* be determined.

Second, since all of the medical evidence (autopsy report, autopsy photographs, written reports, sworn depositions, etc.) are now corrupted and tainted to such an extent, any attempt to introduce them as evidence in a legitimate judicial proceeding would be pointless. In fact, most—if not all—of this evidence would be laughed at and thrown out as inadmissible. Any honest jurist would readily admit this up front; a win-at-all-cost prosecutor probably would not.

Finally, one of the most egregious examples of official misconduct and ineptness in this case was the failure of the local authorities to seal off the scene of the crime. The street where the shooting occurred was immediately open to traffic, and bystanders were allowed to roam freely throughout Dealey Plaza, the adjoining railroad yard and the School Book Depository. The entire crime scene was contaminated and corrupted. We'll never know what evidence might have been collected if this incompetent and disgraceful act had not been permitted.

Of course, this is nowhere near a complete, exhaustive overview of the use, misuse and abuse of the evidence related to this case. That was not our intent. Our intent was to demonstrate the complete and utter impossibility of possessing and examining the requisite factual and reliable evidence and information necessary in order to accurately replicate the Dallas ambush. *It doesn't exist!*

And, as we have now come to realize, none of the evidence, good or bad, would ever be subjected to an adversarial judicial proceeding. There would be no trial because the accused assassin himself was assassinated just two days after the president's murder. Without question, there was a collective sigh of relief on the part of some when Lee Harvey Oswald was executed on live television. Oh, the real killers of John Kennedy were not afraid, as some have presumed, that Oswald might talk. They were fearful of the crime's evidence talking, for the evidence surely would have forcefully cried out, *"Shot from the front!"*

So, in light of this absolute lack of credible evidence, how well do the NatGeo and Discovery documentaries stack up? Their deeply flawed and dishonest presentations brought to remembrance a statement made by the irascible newspaper editor and early Warren Commission critic, Penn Jones Jr. In describing the equally flawed, disinformation publication, the Warren Report, Jones snorted, "The problem with the report is that they forgot to underline where they lied to us."

And, perhaps more telling, Robert Kennedy, JFK's younger brother, and the attorney general of the United States at the time of the assassination, considered the Warren Commission's theory of a single bullet and its conclusion of a lone assassin to be "shoddy work." Or, in a word, bunk!

Unfortunately, the future will undoubtedly bring about other faux "investigative" documentaries noisily proclaiming the sole-assassin invention. The actual perpetrators of this crime, and their whitewash accomplices, may be long gone, but their descendants—as well as some of the neo whitewash artists—are still around. But the people will never fall for their baseless propaganda—they are way smarter than that!

The O'Reilly Non-Factor

One does not necessarily have to think of Bill O'Reilly as being in cahoots with other Kennedy assassination cover-up artists, such as Vincent

Bugliosi, Gerald Posner, Dale Meyers and John McAdams. These "lone nutters" have an agenda with regard to Kennedy's death. They're the self-styled guardians of the fabrication of the lone assassin (Lee Harvey Oswald) and the lone avenger (Jack Ruby). The O'Reilly book *Killing Kennedy* reveals the author to be way too shallow, too self-serving and too self-involved to expend the necessary time, resources and effort truly required to understand the complexities of a violent criminal act. A *huge* investment of time and energy would be required in order to digest and understand the facts surrounding this politically motivated murder; with its subsequent deceitful government-sponsored cover-up. Even then, it would take real courage to tell the truth, the whole truth, and nothing but the truth about that cover-up. But an intensely researched and truthfully written exposé probably would mean no immediate best-seller status and no fast, easy bucks. So don't be too harsh on O'Reilly if he's chosen not to be bothered with such trivial matters as truth and justice. When he had both the platform and the opportunity to do something inordinately great for this country, he elected to look the other way.

And now it's been announced that O'Reilly and NatGeo are teaming up to produce a television special utilizing his superficial and disgracefully insignificant book. Now there's a solid, trustworthy combo for you!

The Pursuit of Truth Persists

Years of excellent research have turned up other sordid details from events that happened after the body left Parkland Memorial Hospital fifty years ago. Some of the autopsy photographs allegedly taken at Bethesda during the autopsy were not taken with the cameras that were used that night. An examination of "Kennedy's brain" was done two weeks after that brain was buried with him at Arlington. At least two of the workers at labs in Washington, DC, where photographs were developed, told the Assassination Records Review Board under oath that the pictures they saw and developed that weekend did not depict the wounds now considered "official" in the Archives. Shamefully, we could compile a much longer list.

If David Lifton and the other medical researchers could grasp the significance of the medical evidence and its contamination, so could the defenders of the Warren Commission and other government inquiries. They knew what was a threat and what was not a threat. Based on a police Dictabelt recording, the HSCA concluded that another gunman—not Oswald—had fired a shot from the infamous grassy knoll. It was a conspiracy—more accurately, a "conspiracy-ette," a mini-conspiracy. Though it was fired from less than ninety feet from the presidential limousine, that shot missed everything: the car, the grass, any spectators, any buildings in Dealey Plaza, everything on earth. That bullet might still be sailing someplace south of Dallas. So said the HSCA. The defenders hardly yawned. That was no threat.

But to suggest that the medical evidence was altered, that hands and scalpels altered wounds, to suggest that a false story of the body was produced and that the Archives contained illegitimate photos and X-rays has been to invite the wrath of our national government. It brought down on Dr. Charles Crenshaw the wrath of *JAMA*, of Lundberg, Breo, even many of Dr. Crenshaw's colleagues at Parkland. To say the medical evidence was altered was anathema to an exponential power. Aiming only to reveal the truth of what he had seen twenty-nine years earlier, Crenshaw had tugged on Superman's cape.

Why the wrath from on high? Refer again to Mr. Lifton and *Best Evidence*. Assume that the body was illegally taken from Dallas, altered, and put back into evidence as a medical forgery. Who had the power and means to do that? Round up the usual suspects, as Captain Louis Renault would say in *Casablanca*. How about . . . Southern segregationists? The Soviets? Castro? The South Vietnamese? The FBI? Organized Crime? Even the multitasking CIA? We think not.

A Colossal Lie Exposed

Not long after Dr. Crenshaw's book had drawn the ire of *JAMA*, JFK researchers got an indication as to how far the guardians of the myth of the lone gunman were willing to go to protect the inviolability of the medical misfit they had created. Past official prevarication and deception essential to safeguard the damaging reality of the autopsy photographs was about to be divulged.

The public uproar generated by Oliver Stone's movie *JFK* forced the release of some of the government's suspiciously suppressed assassination documents. These records, which were thought to have been safely tucked away from public view until 2029, revealed that a congressional investigating committee, the HSCA, had told the American people a colossal lie. For in their previously published report, they had authoritatively declared that the twenty-six people present at the president's autopsy were in disagreement with those Parkland doctors who had described an exit wound in the back of the president's head. These autopsy witnesses, the report stated, had corroborated the general location of the president's wounds as depicted in the autopsy photographs; and, therefore, the observations of the Parkland doctors were incorrect. The truth, however, as revealed in these previously

withheld documents—raw investigative files—
was much different. The twenty-six autopsy
witnesses had, in fact, *agreed* with the Parkland
doctors by diagram and verbal description. *A
medical forgery had been executed.* And, as of
this date, no former HSCA member will admit
authoring this contemptible falsehood. Never-
theless, it appears that the buck has to stop at
the desk of the committee's chief counsel, G.
Robert Blakey.

A medical forgery! *A medical forgery means
involvement by elements of the United States government itself. It means a coup.* Nothing like
the HSCA's shot "seen nowhere in the world."
It means more—then and maybe even now—
than the American people are willing to allow
to have happened. What Dr. Crenshaw saw
in Trauma Room 1 is our ticket to the Dark
Side . . . and we don't want to go.

At The End of the Day

So, in the end, it was the *true* creators of "sad
fabrication based on unsubstantiated allegations," who had been disgracefully exposed
for all to see—and the culprit was *not* Dr.
Charles Crenshaw.

At Dr. Crenshaw's funeral, Brad Kizzia, the attorney who so skillfully and effectively handled
the litigation against *JAMA,* eulogized the

doctor with these words: *"Dr. Crenshaw was a true eyewitness to history. But to me, and those who knew him well, he was a reluctant hero. You see, contrary to what may have been suggested by people who did not actually* know *Dr. Crenshaw, he did not really savor the limelight or seek out publicity. He was not obsessed with the Kennedy assassination. He was not even a conspiracy buff. Rather, he believed he had important information and a unique perspective that should be added to the historical record. . . . His contributions will* not *be forgotten, nor should they be."*

We echo those feelings, and are exceptionally proud and honored to have known and worked with Dr. Charles A. Crenshaw, one who *"stood at a crossroads in history and did not flinch, who faced even stronger forces than he could have known and still dared to speak truth to power"*—to evil power.

3

PERSONAL REFLECTIONS ON
CHARLES CRENSHAW AND THE
JFK ASSASSINATION

Cyril Wecht, M.D., J.D.

I had the opportunity to meet and talk with
Dr. Charles A. Crenshaw shortly after the publication of his book, which in 1992 was entitled
JFK: Conspiracy of Silence. Over the next several
years, we developed a warm, personal friendship that evolved from our strong interest in
exposing the forensic scientific flaws, gross
ineptitude and deliberate attempts to cover
up the truth regarding the JFK assassination.

Charles Crenshaw was a true gentleman in
every respect. He was always gracious, con-
siderate and honest. He was not a wild-eyed
zealot consumed with overwhelming passion,
egotism or a desire to become wealthy and
famous by writing a book in which he demonstrated clearly the absurdity of the Warren Commission Report's (WCR's) conclusion that Lee
Harvey Oswald was a sole assassin. As a matter
of fact, Dr. Crenshaw did not decide to write

this book for more than a quarter of a century following the assassination of the President on Friday, November 22, 1963, in Dallas. At that time, he was well established as a highly respected surgeon in Fort Worth with a very active successful medical practice, a lovely wife and a great number of professional colleagues and personal friends who held him in utmost esteem. For Dr. Crenshaw to have made such a momentous decision to set forth his clear-cut personal recollections of what had transpired at Parkland Hospital Emergency Room, when the president was brought there after being shot in Dealey Plaza, required a tremendous amount of courage, principle and dedication to truth and justice.

I shall always remember the vicious, ruthless and defamatory manner in which Dr. Crenshaw was vilified by Dr. George Lundberg, then editor in chief of the *Journal of the American Medical Association (JAMA).* Lundberg was a personal friend and professional pathology colleague of Dr. Humes's and Dr. Boswell's, the two career military pathologists at Bethesda Naval Hospital who performed the autopsy on JFK that evening. He undertook a campaign against Dr. Crenshaw following the publication of *JFK: Conspiracy of Silence* with unbridled disrespect and ad hominem malevolence. Whether Lundberg made the decision to publish articles in *JAMA* attacking Crenshaw in such a fashion without direction from any individual or group is a fascinating question that we most probably will never know the answer to. In any event, Lundberg assigned a highly unethical writer, Dennis Breo, to write articles claiming that Crenshaw had not even been present in the Parkland Hospital ER when Kennedy was brought there, and that Crenshaw never had any direct involvement of any kind in the treatment of President Kennedy. Breo never interviewed Crenshaw and failed to undertake the most basic journalistic approach and preparation for such articles by examining the official records and learning what various physicians had testified to before the Warren Commission and in subsequent interviews. Had he done so, he would have quickly ascertained that Dr. Crenshaw was indeed present at Parkland Hospital that day and was an active participant in the emergency care of the president.

JAMA articles were never submitted to outside individuals for usual peer review, something that Lundberg was forced to admit under oath in subsequent litigation. After scurrilously attacking Crenshaw and participating in a well-orchestrated national campaign to defame this fine gentleman, Lundberg eventually sealed his own fate. Prominent journalists like Lawrence K. Altman, M.D., *New York Times* writer, and many other veteran investigative journalists undertook an examination of the record and quickly learned quite unequivocally that Dr. Crenshaw had indeed been at Parkland Hospital and was one of the treating physicians, even though he was only a third-year surgical resident at the time. (Among the various physicians who participated in the treatment of President Kennedy that day were other resident physicians, too.)

Dr. Crenshaw's attorney, Bradley Kizzia, Esq., an outstanding lawyer in Dallas and a very knowledgeable expert regarding the JFK assassination, filed a defamation lawsuit against Dr. Lundberg, American Medical Association, and Dennis Breo. Faced with the insurmountable truth, the defendants opted to settle the case for a substantial amount of money rather than defend their dishonesty and grievous breach of journalistic ethics by going to trial.

Dr. Crenshaw and I conducted some news conferences and participated in programs dealing with this sordid affair and discussing the medical and forensic scientific aspects of the JFK assassination following publication of his book. I always admired his ability to articulate these dramatic historical events in a clear, calm, professional fashion. He would patiently listen to other peoples' views and respond in a polite and highly professional fashion.

The opportunity to have developed a warm personal friendship and to have worked in such a professionally collegial fashion with Dr.

Charles A. Crenshaw has undoubtedly been one of the highlights of my long-standing involvement and strong interest in the JFK assassination. Since I first went to the Carnegie Library in Pittsburgh in the late fall of 1964 to look through the twenty-six volumes of the Warren Commission Report's supporting documents, in preparation for my presentation at a plenary session of the American Academy of Forensic Sciences in February 1965, which was dealing with the JFK assassination, I have encountered many highly motivated, well-educated, serious individuals who are critical of the Warren Commission Report. I have spoken on this subject more than a thousand times and participated in hundreds of program throughout the United States and around the world. These endeavors have meant a great deal to me over the past five decades, and I have maintained close personal relationships with great pleasure and much respect. The admiration I feel for all of these dedicated individuals who continue to search for the truth regarding the JFK assassination sustains me in my dark moments of pessimism about whether the unvarnished truth regarding the assassination of President John F. Kennedy will ever be known. Among those cherished memories and warm personal relationships are the feelings I shall always recall and retain in my heart and mind regarding a courageous individual, Dr. Charles A. Crenshaw.

Readers of this new edition, now retitled *JFK Has Been Shot*, will find it easy to understand why the vast community of WCR critic-researchers will always consider Dr. Charles A. Crenshaw as a great American hero.

ABOUT THE AUTHORS

Charles A. Crenshaw, M.D., a Texas native, was the director and chairman of the Department of Surgery of the Tarrant County Hospital District. Educated at Southern Methodist University, East Texas State University, Baylor University Graduate Research Institute, and the University of Texas Southwestern Medical School at Dallas, he interned at Veterans Administration Hospital and completed his residency at Dallas's Parkland Memorial Hospital, where he worked for five years. He taught at UT Southwestern Medical School and served on the staffs of John Peter Smith Hospital and St. Joseph Hospital, both in Fort Worth, and Parkland Memorial Hospital. He was active in the Tarrant County Cancer Society and other organizations devoted to public health. Dr. Crenshaw was named chairman emeritus of the Department of Surgery of John Peter Smith Hospital, where he was a member of the teaching staff for twenty-eight years. He was appointed to the hospital's Board of Managers in 1998. He was honored with inclusion in numerous medical and professional societies.

Jens Hansen is a writer and petroleum land manager who earned a B.A. in history at Texas Tech University in Lubbock and did postgraduate work at North Texas State University.

J. Gary Shaw is a retired architect and a forty-five-plus-year researcher/critic of the JFK assassination investigation and conclusions. He is a former director of the JFK Assassination Information Center in Dallas and the Assassination Archives and Research Center in Washington, DC. He is considered one of the world's leading authorities on the John F. Kennedy assassination and is the author of a previous book on the subject, *Cover-Up: The Governmental Conspiracy to Conceal the Facts About the Public Execution of John Kennedy.*

Robert K. Tanenbaum is a nationally known attorney and legal expert and a New York Times bestselling author. He is one of the country's most respected trial lawyers and has never lost a felony case.

Born in Brooklyn, New York, Tanenbaum attended the University of California at Berkeley on a basketball scholarship. He received his law degree from Boalt Hall School of Law at the University of California, Berkeley. At the outset of his distinguished career, he was an Assistant D.A. in New York County, where he ran the Homicide Bureau, served as Chief of the Criminal Courts, and was in charge of the D.A.'s legal staff training program. Mel Glass, John Keenan, and D.A. Frank Hogan were his esteemed mentors, and *Echoes of My Soul* is a tribute to them, written at the request of Mel Glass with his active involvement. Tanenbaum was appointed Deputy Chief Counsel for the Congressional committee investigations into the assassinations of President John F. Kennedy and Dr. Martin Luther King, Jr. For four years he taught Advanced Criminal Procedure at his alma mater, Boalt Hall School of Law. He served two terms as Mayor of Beverly Hills. A popular media guest, he regularly appears on television shows as a legal commentator. He is the author of 25 Butch Karp thrillers and three non-fiction books, including *The Piano Teacher: The True Story of a Psychotic Killer* and *Badge of the Assassin*. His latest novel is *Tragic*.

Cyril H. Wecht, M.D., J.D., is a forensic pathologist, attorney and medical-legal consultant. He received his medical degree from the University of Pittsburgh, and his law degree from the University of Maryland. Dr. Wecht is certified by the American Board of Pathology and is a Fellow of the College of American Pathologists and the American Society of Clinical

Pathologists. He is a Clinical Professor at the University of Pittsburgh School of Medicine and Graduate School of Public Health; an Adjunct Professor at the Duquesne University School of Law, School of Pharmacy, and School of Health Sciences; and Distinguished Professor of Pathology at Carlow University. He has served as President of the American College of Legal Medicine, the American Academy of Forensic Sciences, and served as Chairman of the Board of Trustees of the American Board of Legal Medicine and the American College of Legal Medicine Foundation. The author of more than 575 professional publications, Dr. Wecht is also the author of *From Crime Scene to Courtroom, A Question of Murder, Tales From the Morgue, Mortal Evidence, Cause of Death, Grave Secrets,* and *Who Killed JonBenet Ramsey?*

Formerly the Chairman of the Department of Pathology at Saint Francis Central Hospital in Pittsburgh, Dr. Wecht has performed approximately 18,000 autopsies and has supervised, reviewed, or has been consulted on approximately 38,000 additional postmortem examinations.

Dr. Wecht has frequently appeared on nationally syndicated programs to discuss the assassinations of President John F. Kennedy and Senator Robert F. Kennedy, the death of Elvis Presley, the O.J. Simpson case, and the JonBenet Ramsey case. His expertise has also been called upon in high-profile cases involving Laci Peterson, Chandra Levy, Mary Jo Kopechne, Sunny von Bulow, Jean Harris, Dr. Jeffrey McDonald, the Waco Branch Davidian fire, and Vincent Foster. Please visit his website, www.cyrilwecht.com.

Island of Promise

MADELEINE CARR

API Books

Copyright © 1982 by Madeleine Carr

Reprinted under licence by permission of

River Publishing Co., Inc.
149 Fifth Avenue - Suite 1301
New York, NY 10010

Printed in Canada

ISBN: 1-55547-328-8

First Printing July 1994